Power, Beauty and Legitimacy of Adolescence

Understanding the teenage period.
From its complexity in reality to some
fictional representations in Anglo-
Saxon, French and Italian literature.

Susan Jane Broda Tamburi

Clink
Street

London | New York

Published by Clink Street Publishing 2019

Copyright © 2019

First edition.

ISBNs:
978-1-912850-84-6 paperback
978-1-912850-85-3 ebook

I dedicate this book to Joyce and Giovanni who have been the best parents ever and to my wonderful four children, Lloyd, Kelly, Scott and Stella. I would also like to thank my loving partner Eugene, whose personal views on education motivated me to express my own and all the teenagers that I have encountered during my teaching years who have been, each in their own way, a great inspiration for my work.

CONTENTS

INTRODUCTION

"L'adolescent ne laisse un bon souvenir qu'aux adultes ayant mauvaise mémoire."

— *François Truffaut*

The famous French film director, screenwriter and producer said that only people with bad memory remembered their adolescence as being carefree.

I have worked for more than twenty-five years with teenagers. Being a teacher to students aged between fifteen and twenty-two, I have been able to observe and analyse their behaviour in detail. After such a long period of time, I feel extremely close to them. What used to amaze, astonish or even shock me at first does not anymore. I find their sometimes weird and rash reactions not only foreseeable and understandable but in some cases moving. Adolescents have won me over so to speak, so much so that I want to become their advocate in helping them being understood by their parents. I have written this book, on the one hand, to help parents in the management of their relationship with their teenagers, giving them a road map to follow, and on the other hand, to share with them a few fictional representations of youth in literature. The final objective being to give adults a few very simple guidelines that will show them how to become efficient parents. The main idea is for mothers and fathers to embrace this wonderful moment in life which is very often badly understood or handled and equally apprehended by the teenagers themselves. Ultimately it is about creating a lifelong relationship with maturing children based on love, respect, understanding and collaborative construction.

PART I

DEALING WITH
THE TEENAGE YEARS

1

WHAT IS ADOLESCENCE?

UNDERSTANDING TEENAGERS

How to handle a teenager is an ongoing problem. The world changes, behaviours evolve, but the passage from childhood to adulthood is a perennial issue. Our children all go through a stage in their life which is critical and every parent is, one day or another, confronted to the problem of managing this troublesome period called adolescence. The etymology of the word comes from the Latin *adolescere*: growing and *alere*: to nurture, to make something grow. Adolescence corresponds to the period of life between puberty and adulthood. It is a journey that will bring the individual a greater autonomy having gone through a process of growing, learning and maturing. It is interesting to know that according to the UNICEF 2016 statistics, the teenage population was estimated at 1.8 billion, the largest adolescent population that the world has ever known.

In English, the term teenagers includes ages from thirteen to nineteen. But nowadays it seems that the period of adolescence is much longer and more flexible. Studies have shown that young people reach puberty much earlier and, as socioeconomic reasons push them to live at home over a longer period of time, the coexistence between parents and teens can last quite a few years.

Let's go back in time to fully understand the situation that teenagers face today. Their status has greatly changed over the years. In Europe, children of fourteen and even younger often left their homes to work for other families or to start an apprenticeship. In the 19th century the situation changed because of industrialisation and more and more teenagers stayed at home and worked to help the household financially up to the age of their wedding. Then in the 20th century, three main changes occurred; child protection laws, compulsory schooling and longer school years. These three elements meant that children were going to spend much more time in the home. Consequently, young people found themselves in a situation in which they became financially dependent on their parents. This was also enhanced by the fact that families became less numerous and that dwellings were getting bigger. Economic reasons linked to increasing unemployment are added factors which pushed teenagers and adults to live under the same roof. Up to this day, many young adults just can't afford to pay their own lodgings. The whole family dynamics is thus altered and parents have to find ways to adapt to this unsettling situation.

Dealing with adolescence is difficult but it is also a wonderful opportunity to do things right and to ensure a good and healthy relationship between two generations. This challenge can be either constructive or very damaging for everyone concerned, seriously jeopardising the future adult to adult relationship. Instead of just reacting or overreacting to teenagers' behaviour one has to adopt a philosophical approach to bring harmony back in the family. One needs practical tools to achieve this but it is mainly about taking on a drastically new attitude.

I have a way of solving problems which came quite instinctively to me when my children started to become teenagers. My method was consolidated and made stronger thanks to my professional and personal experience as well as my constant documentation on the subject. Over the years, my approach was repeatedly reinforced by multiple contacts with colleagues, friends, students and parents.

My natural empathy and analytical frame of mind seem to encourage people to confide in me when they are faced with problems of all sorts, including those related to education. Each time a case is presented to me, I realise that it is the same misunderstanding that triggers off a bad relationship and strong tensions between the parents and the children. Although some situations seem deadlocked, there is always a key at hand.

My approach is extremely simple and goes against educational systems based on authority or stiff hierarchy. There are two preliminary conditions: firstly, a full understanding of what an adolescent is going through, not only physically but psychologically, and secondly the unequivocal will on the parents' side to adopt an adequate personal behaviour. The final objective being to reconcile parents and teenagers and to restore the good relationship that existed between them previously.

One has to realise that the teenagers are in a middle of a bridge which is connecting childhood to adulthood. In order for the youths to manage to cross it peacefully and to prevent them from either getting lost in the middle of it or jumping off, the adult will have to accompany them step by step to the other side thus allowing them to continue life harmoniously. As we shall see the adolescent will need a loving guide, and that guide is you. But it's the nature of the guidance that will have to be appropriate because there are many traps best-intentioned parent may well fall into.

David le Breton, anthropologist and professor of sociology at the university of Strasbourg uses a similar image in his book *In Suffering. Adolescence and Entrance into Life* (2007):

> Even if the human condition always remains unachieved and therefore in a kind of 'adolescens', the passage to the other side represents a farewell to childhood, and the fact that now one is the author of one's own existence. During the period between these two worlds which is, as it were, a prelude to manhood or womanhood, the youth is simultaneously in search of his autonomy but without wanting to cut himself from the guardianship of his surrounding, he thus experiments for the best or for the worst his status of subject, the frontier between the within and the without, plays with social bans and tests his place within a world in which he doesn't really recognise himself.

I am going to show how to accompany teenagers, step by step, and consequently modify the tense relationship that often prevails between the two generations at such a time. This implies from the part of the adult both humility and a capacity of careful listening, two qualities that are sometimes missing.

The very first thing one has to acknowledge is that, in a conflictual relationship between a parent and a teenager, there are two entities and not only one. It is the alchemy between the two behaviours which poses a problem because not only does the parent find it difficult or even impossible to put up with the youth's conduct but the adolescent is at a stage in which he or she can't stand the ways of the parent either and of society itself to some degree. To be clear, the behaviour of the adult must always be "in tune" as Françoise Dolto, the famous French paediatrician and psychoanalyst would say, to enable the youths to navigate safely their way out of this difficult period. This requires self-control on the part of the adults but also readiness to question the appropriateness of their responses on a regular basis. The attitude of the adult will be paramount because it will either pacify or aggravate matters. Ultimately, as I shall demonstrate, it is a struggle of power and control that is going on and for the parents to win it, they first have to lose it. We shall see how the most effective parents are those who thoughtfully surrender control. The aim being that any idea of overruling is finally abandoned, leading to a win–win situation.

An analysis of the problems of adolescence has to be considered in the context of its interaction with the external world, that is the parents, teachers, but also the social and professional environment. Therefore not only shall I show the specificity of adolescence but also, and foremost, I shall underline the proper reactions and attitude adults, teachers and professional trainers have to have when dealing with youths. If we, as adults, have properly overcome our own adolescence and if we have reached some degree of wisdom, we should be able to manage this task successfully.

Very few parents who feel lost and disarmed facing their boisterous teens have the will or the financial means to ask for the help of a mediator, who could easily help them with adequate counselling. Therefore, the great majority of parents find themselves in the tricky situation of being at the same time the mediator and one of the actors in the conflict. This double role is very difficult to play. Consequently, the resolution of the problem is practically impossible. Self-reflexion should be the very start of this new way to go about living with a teenager. The only way to manage this complex task is to have a very objective view of the behaviour of the two parties, the youth's and the adult's. Teenagers and parents have to learn from one another in a constructive way.

What I would like to point out is the interdependence of parents' and teens' reactions. Because both influence one another constantly, the parents need to take care of themselves to make sure they can deal with their children. If they want teenagers to respect them, they have to respect them too. If parents expect self-control from their children they have to demonstrate it. Let's keep in mind at all times that children are a precious gift we have been given. As time goes on, their maturity is bound to catch up with ours and we shall be able to meet on common grounds as adults. This is the best proof that things have been done well by parents during the twenty or so years in which they have prepared their children for life.

PHYSICAL AND PSYCHOLOGICAL TRANSFORMATIONS

But when does adolescence really begin? The period seems to be more flexible than many people may think. Puberty varies from one person to another and starts earlier for a girl than a boy. Before puberty we also distinguish one or two years which are called pubescence. There is an unequal repartition of the age of puberty according to geographical regions, climate and genome, that is the complete set of genetic material present in a cell. In the Mediterranean and tropical regions, it occurs between nine and eleven years of age, whereas in the Northern regions it is more around fourteen to seventeen and in the Temperate Zones, puberty starts between eleven and thirteen.

Recent studies have been carried out on a relatively new phenomenon called *early onset of puberty*. This is triggered by external factors and apparently affects more girls than boys. Very interesting conclusions were made public at the Rencontres Santé Publique France, a conference organised in Paris in 2017. Indeed, the results of a study that was made between 2011 and 2013 showed that in France 1173 new cases of early puberty for girls and ten times less for boys were found. The cause of this phenomenon seems to be the endocrine disruptors, toxic chemicals that can interfere with the hormonal system. The long-term contact with dangerous substances alter the body of children thus changing their behaviour accordingly, with mood swings and various other problems within the family and school.

Puberty marks the beginning of adolescence but must not be mistaken with the mere fact of growing. This period which shatters childhood landmarks is much more unsettling. Dealing with this disruption is going to prove extremely challenging for the youth who has to deal with intense physical changes. A huge hormonal kick-in is going to start a chain reaction and induce new urges. Physical changes which are ultimately positive will be accompanied by perturbing elements going from slight skin affections to overweight. Teenagers are going to question themselves of how to fit in their new body. Although parents are obviously aware that changes are occurring in their children, many don't realise how profound they are, principally because their new intimacy will be visible from the outside before the teenager has had time to integrate the metamorphoses mentally. Coping with this new identity will have both emotional and cognitive impacts and adults have to consider the phenomenon as a whole.

In order to have a better idea of what one is dealing with, let's see what science actually tells us about this period of physical development. It is the endocrine system which sets off puberty. One has to distinguish two different stages: the maturing of adrenal glands, and later on the maturing of sexual glands. But physical and hormonal changes begin well before these two stages. Around the age of eight years old when the adrenal glands produce higher rate levels of hormones, the hypothalamus, a region of the brain which directs part of the nervous system and regulates hormonal cycles, signals the pituitary glands to release gonadotropins in the bloodstream. These hormones come about one year before the bodily changes begin. We then have oestrogen production and androgen production by the ovaries (girls) and testes (boys).

If we refer to the maturity scale established by the British paediatrician James M. Tanner in 1962, we can distinguish on the one hand the primary sexual characteristics which are directly linked to the reproductive system and organs and the secondary ones which include all the changes which are not directly related to the reproductive function, for example, facial hair, broader shoulders and mutation in the voice for boys and breast development and widening pelvic bones for girls. Puberty is the point at which sexual organs mature. As puberty goes on, these hormonal changes can also induce distress, hostility or even, in some cases, mild to deep depression.

Psychological impacts are going to be numerous. Whether it is the first period experienced by young girls (menarche) or the first nocturnal emission for the young boys, there are going to be, for both genders, many physical adaptations that will impact them psychologically. Most teenagers will find these transformations worrying. Although all of them will not resent these, many will fear not being in the norm and will feel they are not in control of the changes happening to their body. The anxiety that these changes induce will not only have to be acknowledged but fully understood by the parents. Empathy, as we shall see, will be of crucial importance here. Parents will have to restrain from all inadequate judgment which could have extremely bad effects on the teenager's self-concept. Later on, we shall differentiate the two notions of self-concept and self-esteem which are of utmost importance at this stage.

I often use the example of two identical drawings, one on a sheet of paper and the other on translucent paper laid on top. During adolescence, it is as though the paper was moved and that the lines of the drawings didn't coincide anymore. Once the troublesome period is over, the two designs are aligned just as they were at the beginning. It is an adaptation that takes some significant time, it can occur more or less rapidly, but is never automatic. The youth has to face and moreover integrate this new body which is showing signs of puberty and sexual inclinations. Adjustments will have to be made both in changes in appearance and in bodily urges. At the same time, the teen has to become autonomous and start living and thinking for his or her own sake. This change entails a repositioning of all his entourage, and obviously, parents are in the first position.

Physical transformations can therefore cause doubts, fears and psychological readjustments as well as a general feeling of imbalance. Physiological and morphological changes also have a direct effect on self-image. This will all lead to the final integration of adult personality which, chronologically, follows the periods of conflict and adjustments. As I will show later on, one will have to avoid any kind of criticism and will have to show understanding at all times.

Parents will have to remember that the young adults are, as Françoise Dolto put it, "fragile like moulting lobsters" that their flesh is exposed and vulnerable, and they are in search of their own identity. The *lobster complex* is an expression she invented in 1989 in her book *Paroles pour adolescents ou Le complexe du homard*. It represents the adolescent crisis as a whole. 'The child will rid himself of his or her carapace, suddenly too tight to find another one. In the meantime, he or she is vulnerable, aggressive or introvert.' However, 'what will appear,' she continues, 'is the product of what was sown by the adults when he or she was a child.' Insisting on the influence of the parents' behaviour, Dolto concludes:

> The parents should therefore expect the barriers to explode, these barriers being flexible enough to let go at the right moment. On the contrary, if the parents were too rigid in the education of their young child, when becoming a teenager, the individual will be prisoner of his or her carapace and disarmed when faced with depression or anxiety.

Thus teenagers will use this period to experiment with their body. Sometimes in shocking ways. But as Dolto points out, they should be recognised the right to learn how to own their physical image by experimenting with their appearance. As we shall see later on, any kind of undue or awkward remark concerning their physical appearance could have devastating consequences.

Today young people are in quest of the perfect body which makes things even more problematic. Not only are they exposed right and left to pictures of flawless bodies and faces in social media but also to instant messaging services such as Snapchat and other apps which allow them to Photoshop their own appearance to send out a perfect image of themselves. The amount of cosmetic surgery performed on teenagers has exploded in the past few years, interventions that were formerly confined to adults, are now carried out on young bodies and faces at an extravagantly early age. Unrealistic goals feed the anxiety that is already naturally present at adolescence, making things even harder to deal with. Exponential dissatisfaction with their own appearance is more and more frequent, fuelled by reality shows putting forward young people who have practically all experienced some kind of physical alteration from heavy cosmetic surgery or contouring to lighter dermatological procedures.

The somatic changes that are linked to puberty are numerous. This period is a high risk one. Just as a baby has to discover a corporeal and sensorial universe through different stages of his development, the adolescent will have to accept his or her new physical frame. This physical development goes hand in hand with psycho-affective changes. Not only will the puberty process impose on the adolescent an effort of appropriation of a new body but will also impose a new social status. This explains why numerous parents complain about the egoism and egotism of their youths, forgetting that this centralisation is not only normal but necessary. Teenagers have to be self-centred because they are trying to unravel information about themselves and are simultaneously attempting to set their own values.

SELF-CONCEPT AND SELF-ESTEEM

At this stage, it is important to differentiate two notions: self-concept and self-esteem. Psychologists Carl Rogers and Abraham Maslow had a major influence in popularising the idea of self-concept. According to Rogers, everyone strives to reach an "ideal-self". One's self-concept is a collection of beliefs about oneself. It is the answer to the question "Who am I?" The notion of self-concept is also called self-structure, self-perspective, self-identity or self-construction. Whereas self-concept is a cognitive or descriptive component of one's self (*I'm pretty*), self-esteem is evaluative and opinionated (*I feel good about being pretty*). One's self-concept is made up of self-schemas, and their past, present and future selves. By future selves, one has to understand possible selves, that is what they might become, what they would like to become or what they are afraid of becoming.

The establishment of self-concept takes place very early in life. What the parents imply or say about their young child will have direct repercussions on the way they feel about themselves.

Adolescents experience significant changes in general physical self-concept, at the onset of puberty. They are weakened by the significant physical changes in conjunction with the psychological adaptations they have to make during this period. Therefore, self-concept is at its lowest in adolescents because they are struggling in understanding such a new flow of information. So many things are happening to them concomitantly. Every time they look at their body they have to make adjustments. 'What should I look like? Is this normal? What other changes are going to happen? Am I attractive? Do I want to be attractive?'

Paradoxically, a teenager who is experiencing self-doubt often adopts a defensive behaviour and pretends to be in control. This attitude does not however bear close examination, it is obvious that any excessively cool behaviour often dissimulates profound doubts and insecurities.

To build self-concept in their children, parents have to provide both stated and unstated messages that show their unconditional love and support. Formulating or implying notions like 'I value you' and acting to prove it, is the best way to achieve this. As importantly, parents have to provide both stated and unstated messages that give the following message: 'You can think for yourself, you have control, you can own your decisions *and* I trust you.' Unfortunately, too many parents keep on putting their finger on what the teenager does wrong and presenting themselves as perfect models to be imitated. On the contrary, parents have to help teens become aware of their strengths and build from there.

Unstated or covert messages are powerful. When parents imply that their teen is able to do something, they actually manage to handle it. Day after day, this builds up their self-concept. Similarly, as I will point out later in the analysis, if a teacher makes the students understand that they can achieve a task they will probably perform very well, if a teacher implies that the students are no good in such or such a domain, their performance will be poor.

Once the adolescents have a strong self-concept, they will be able to make decisions, own them and accept their consequences. This is how they will learn how to be responsible. By telling adolescents what to do, you deprive them of the capability of being responsible. The youths have to make their own choices even if they are wrong, the outcome will soon show them the way to go. The proof that an adult is psychologically healthy is the fact that he or she has finally moved away from roles created by others' expectations and instead looks within himself or herself for validation. We then get the full circle.

BRAIN TRANSFORMATION

Granville Stanley Hall, who was the founder of the movement of child behaviour observation at the beginning of the 20th century, was already aware of the strange structure of the adolescent brain. He implied that imagination was a characteristic of the adolescent period, showing that any crazy or original idea could only come from a young brain. He also showed that such euphoric creativity was very often coupled with high-risk behaviour, changes of mood, impulsivity and obvious lack of discerning.

In psychology, impulsivity or impulsiveness is a tendency to act on a whim, displaying behaviour characterised by little or no forethought as well as no reflection or consideration of the consequences. It is a major component to mental disorders such as ADHD (attention deficit hyperactivity disorder), bipolar disorder and others. Abnormal patterns of impulsivity have also been noted in instances of acquired brain injury and neurodegenerative diseases.

Here, we are talking about temporary adolescent impulsiveness which can be seen two ways. On the one hand parents can criticise their teen's rash decisions when the result is undesirable or dangerous, on the other, if their impulsive actions have positive outcomes, they tend to see their teenagers as bold, quick, spontaneous or courageous.

It is not the outcome of such behaviour that should monitor our acceptance of it. Impulsivity is a facet of the teenage period and whether good or bad it has to be accepted as such. Therefore, what would differentiate an adolescent from an adult is a certain instability but also a richness of personality. The person's profusion would be like a promise of a creative and richly imaginative adult-to-be. We shall see, later in the analysis, that this spontaneity linked to adolescence has to be encouraged and praised but must also be under observance and control. Great creators, artists or geniuses seem to withhold the richness and unbridled energy of adolescence which make them wonderfully imaginative and creative.

Stanley Hall also claimed that the adolescent brain was 'a soil in which a good or bad seed could take root very deep and very fast.' This statement takes on a whole new meaning today with all the youths who let themselves be indoctrinated to commit crimes at an incredibly early age. It is also shocking to know that 40% of adolescents in the world do not benefit from higher education precisely at the age when any educational or social influence has the best chances to be solidly imprinted.

This permeability of the young brain also means that the influence of the entourage is going to be decisive. That is why parents have to be extremely positive during this period of time, in order to optimise the chances of their child's harmonious development.

Some scientific notions have to be clarified. Recent research on the human brain has put into light fundamental insights for the comprehension of what happens to the teenager's brain. A full understanding of these new discoveries obliges us, as parents, to adjust our opinion, attitude and behaviour. It is impossible to have the right reactions if we do not understand the scientific facts which explain why young people behave the way they do.

The brain undergoes a process of restructuring and development that can explain the aberrations of teenage behaviour and their gradual transition to maturity. Since the works of Swiss epistemologist and psychologist Jean Piaget on cognitive development conducted in the early 20th century, it was thought that brain development and its functions were more or less completed around the age of twelve. Indeed, it is true that by then the brain has reached its final size. But with the incredible progress of medical imagery, it is now clear that the maturation of the brain is incomplete until the age of twenty and even twenty-five!

As Dr Frances E. Jensen explains in detail in *The Teenage Brain* (2015), the frontal lobes, just behind the forehead, are the most important zone of the human brain. That is where all the actions are assessed, situations are thought out and decisions are taken. However, the most important element to consider is that this cerebral zone is the last one which actually develops. It is as though all the wirings were not finished. Adolescents lose 15% of grey matter while the white matter increases (the grey matter contains cell bodies and the white matter has the role of connecting the different parts of the grey matter to each other). A process of neural pruning alters the number of connections or synapses between them. According to the works of Dr Jay Giedd, an American child and adolescent psychiatrist, the cabling of its white substance – the sheath of the neurones – which insures the conduction of nervous influx does not get to maturity before the age of twenty years on average.

However, as soon as puberty starts, that is around twelve years of age, and sometimes even a little earlier, the hormonal function is already working at full blast. The hormones that are liberated in the blood circulation affect the neurones belonging to the part of the brain which is related to emotions. This has a direct effect on the behaviour, making the individual want to affirm himself and be taken seriously. There is therefore an incredible discrepancy between urges that push young people to take risks and act without real consideration of danger and maturing of the brain which would enable them to evaluate these same risks. It is not surprising that the two first causes of death in the adolescent population are suicide and road accidents. Adolescents find themselves in the very uncomfortable situation of experiencing bewildering contradictory feelings regarding emancipation. As for the parents, they have the uncomfortable task of dealing with a rash teenager who wants to be considered as a mature adult.

INITIATION RITES

This alchemy between the risks that the young people expose themselves to in the challenges they set themselves and the desire of validation of a sought maturity, is illustrated in initiation rites that can be found in many cultures around the world. The very fact that so many ethnic groups prepare their youngsters for adulthood is the very proof that the passage from one stage to another is not automatic, that it needs to be recognised, legitimised and channelled. The very meaning of the term initiation indicates that the teenagers have to pass a threshold, having to prove something to be accepted in a given social group.

In our complex, multicultural, but nevertheless rigid society, there is a severe risk for teenagers to drift and become marginal. This is caused by their lack of belonging as well as the absence of significant positive encounters and influences in their surroundings. Many wander in a no-man's land, having lost any sense of group. Yet, the process of separation and aggregation is the very essence of adolescence. It's about leaving a number of set structures to evolve and reach another set of values and in the process being awarded recognition based on new criteria of acceptance.

The famous ethnologist Arnold van Gennep published *The Rites of Passage* in 1909. In this book he analyses all kinds of transitions from one stage to another: birth, adolescence, marriage and death. He also describes other cultural rituals referring to key moments in life. To summarise, rites of passage are divided into three stages: first there is separation, that is isolation of the novices from society, then a period of difficult and challenging trials and finally a period of rebirth and adhesion to another group. What is relevant for our analysis is that the period of mutation is never denigrated or criticised. Not only is it anticipated but also highly celebrated.

Religious rituals such as communions or confirmations have lost their original meaning and are often reduced to a family gathering around a meal after the church celebration. Changes are imposed on children who do not always understand the underlying meaning of such festivities.

The transition from childhood to adulthood is celebrated by the Quinceaneras in South America and among Latino immigrants in other countries. The term comes from two Spanish words: *quince* (fifteen) and *años* (years). It is a celebration of girls' transition from childhood to womanhood.

It has cultural roots in Mesoamerica. Historically in the years prior to the fifteenth birthday, girls were taught cooking, weaving and about childbearing by elder women in their communities. In some South American countries such as Argentina, Peru, Bolivia, Ecuador and Uruguay, we can also find the fifteen year candle ceremony which follows the ball. The girl hands a candle to each of the fifteen people that she considers having been the most influential in her life. She often makes a speech to each one of them and expresses her gratitude for helping her during the first part of her life. In French Guinea and in the Caribbeans, the celebration is quite similar and is called Fête des Quinze Ans.

The deeper significance of this ceremony is that the girl is capable of independence in that she can make her own decisions, and it symbolises her transition into womanhood. It also reaffirms her beliefs in her personal faith. In the United States the Sweet Sixteen has the same significance. The regions of Northern Europe have developed some nonreligious ceremonies like the Jungendweihe in Germany which occurs when the child is thirteen years of age.

The Amish youth period called the Rumspringa or "Running around" is a period in which youngsters of sixteen are offered the opportunity of living a few days without any surveillance, far from their families. This period of time is marked by an increase of social activities. They are encouraged to make the most of what they like, be it modern clothing, alcohol or up-to-date technology. The aim is to enable the young Amish to have the opportunity of seeing or discovering the world beyond their culture or education. This means that if the Amish children come back, it will be their own choice. They are then baptised and totally engaged into the community. Rumspringa is a formative time for youths at the end of which they have to choose if they want to join the church or not and enter a more formalised world and peer interaction. For some, it is an angst-filled period of existential choice for others it is a time to find a marriage partner. Extreme behaviours would involve sinful exploration of the world, other much tamer ones, would involve joining social games or dating. Although all Amish parents don't encourage their youth to leave home and experience the world, they are not supposed to condemn it either. In all cases, the adolescents are given an opportunity for making their own choices and decisions and their life will change accordingly.

In the Inuit community, there is an interesting ritual in Baffin Island. The boys aged between eleven and twelve leave the villages and accompany their fathers in the wilderness to test their hunting skills and their climatic adaptation to very low Arctic temperatures. According to their tradition, a shaman is asked to come and open communication access between men and animals. Today this tradition has been adapted and extended to young girls, with the transmission of tasks judged as more feminine, passed on from generation to generation.

In Vanuatu, a little island in the middle of the South Pacific, young boys jump from a wooden scaffolding-like tower of ninety-two meters with a liana attached to their ankle. It is called Gol or "land diving". The danger of this challenge makes the young men very proud when they dare go through with it. They are then automatically accepted in the group of male adults.

In the Apache tradition, young girls would take part in a ceremony of Sundown. This celebration was organised the summer following their first menstruation and lasted four days. The young girls were isolated from their families and had to achieve rituals to be able to be considered as women. In 1883 the US adopted the Code of Indian Offenses which banned many Native American ceremonies. For a long time, such celebrations were conducted in secret. Today, Native Americans have variations of the coming-of-age ritual, depending on the tribe they belong to. For the most part, girls and boys are separated from the tribe and spend several days alone fasting in order to focus on their goal which is to have a dream or a vision. Rituals are performed in circles that represent the never-ending cycle or growth. The number 4 is omnipresent because it represents the four stages: the baby, the child, the adolescent and the adult. The ribbon cutting is performed in some tribes. The teen is attached to the parent, usually the mother by a ribbon of about six feet, gently tied to their wrist. At some point, they have to cut the ribbon and the parent makes a speech. Here is a typical example of one from a Native American mother to her daughter.

I brought you into this world and our spirits will be for-ever joined.
However, up until this time, I have led you through life and you have listened to everything I said.

If you are ready, then today our relationship changes and I offer my guidance and ever-lasting love but know that you have started down your own path and may not always listen.

I do hope our relationship is one of trust, honesty and warmth.
You can cut away our old relationship today, but I will always be here for you.

All these celebrations instil good values and morals and at the same time strengthen and consolidate cultural traditions. It is reassuring to see that all across the United States, there is renewed interest in anything to do with such ancestral traditions.

The Maasai tribe in Africa follow the same idea, their rite of passage is one of the most important East African festivals. It marks the coming-of-age of Maasai boys who are twelve to twenty-five years old. The planning of the ceremony takes two months. It is composed of three distinct periods: the separation stage, in which the boys leave their parents and live in a secluded tent, and have their faces painted. Traditionally they also had to show their courage by killing a lion. The second stage is when they are circumcised to become men, they then spend four to eight months dressed in black which symbolises their spiritual transition. Finally, the third stage is the incorporation or readmittance into the society of warriors. They then have the responsibility of protecting their village and are honoured and respected.

Closer to us, we have scouting, created by Robert Baden-Powell in 1907, a British retired general, who had always been interested in questions of education and the involvement of youth. He synthesised all the documentation he had read and the experience he had gone through to eventually come up with a youth movement with its intrinsic characteristics. His own teenage period was a great inspiration for him because he was told of the adventures of his grandfather the admiral William Henry Smith and another one of his ancestors, John Smyth, who had crossed the state of Virginia, which was still unexplored at that point.

The young Robert practised sailing with his brothers and thus learnt about such notions as the importance of shared responsibilities on board, survival, helping others and other basic human values. Scouting was founded on a pedagogical principle which seeks to give responsibility to a youth to shape his character by ludic activities and by concrete action involving nature and the outdoors. The aim being to become a better person following traditional values. All this was very beneficial as adolescents were given an objective to follow which distanced them from dangerous marginality or isolation.

Scouting is represented today by more than forty million members in 217 countries and lands of all religions and nationalities. However, this movement is more and more endangered by the modern way of life. Nowadays, young people lose themselves in an online world made of solitude, with so-called *friends* or *followers* that are only virtual. They are up-to-date with technology but estranged from reality and nature. The internet has substituted the outdoors. Such inactivity and idleness has terrible consequences. Our growing children need to know that there are some fundamental values that have to be transmitted from generation to generation and they need the older generation to hand these down to them. Rituals and rites are being lost when they are needed the most.

Recently, the French Government, which felt powerless due to growing terrorism and street violence, has decided to motivate its teenagers, suggesting that they take part in some kind of compulsory civic engagement for a few weeks (known as service national universel), which is a way to give a sense to their life and a direction to people who are very often lost, and who would, given a chance, follow any kind of destructive ideology. The young people who live in the suburbs of big towns like Paris, Lyon or Marseille have neither moral guidance nor objectives. They have to struggle in a world that rejects them by mere prejudice. They are caught in a vicious circle of school failure and stigmatisation which leads to a downward spiral made of drugs, violence and radicalism.

2

PARENTING

COMMON MISTAKES PARENTS MAKE

Thorough understanding of teenagers' behaviour requires a careful analysis of its motivations and complexity.

The first great mistake is to consider adolescence as an isolated moment in the evolution of the individual, a critical period which would be completely different from previous ones. Not only do teenagers have a history which greatly determines their reactions to the events they are currently experiencing, but the period they are living is as outstanding as other stages of their childhood life, like weaning or autonomy in corporeal hygiene, walking, speaking or reading.

All these stages are also crises that are experienced naturally and harmoniously by most children in caring families but, in some cases, can also pose problems. Potty training, walking, and speaking are processes which are not equally experienced by every child. Careful coaching by parents and by the child's entourage is determining. In the Ceaușescu era, films of Romanian orphanages showed us shocking footage of children who were profoundly retarded precisely because they had been denied the necessary stimulation and incentive at each stage of their development.

Therefore, adolescence is not to be seen as a crisis in the negative sense of the term but in the sense in which it is used in psychology: a critical moment which will have important consequences on the development of an individual both physiologically and psychologically. A moment of drastic change that needs attention, just like the one that would be given to the first steps or the first spoken words of a toddler.

The fact that a teens are older than children and that they often reject any kind of counselling or advice should not deter parents from giving them as much, if not more, focus and guidance.

According to the famous German-American developmental psychologist Erik Erikson, 'Adolescence should be seen as a specific vulnerability linked to an unbalance provoked by the development of new potentials in the individual.'

The expression *teenage crisis* is therefore a terminology which could induce us in error because it seems to refer to something which is negative whereas it is a change towards something positive. Instead of saying 'My teen is going through a crisis' one should say 'My teen is becoming an adult.' The second wording is much more valorising and respectful. It should not be seen any more as a problematic period that literally hits a growing child and affects the whole family but a mere normal and natural evolution of the individual that needs adequate response. This progression should not only be welcomed but embraced by all the members of the family.

Other developmental psychologists like James E. Marcia go even further in their analysis. They defend the idea that 'the process of identity does not start or stop with adolescence.' This means that adults are still going through other experiences which can modify and consolidate the establishment of their own identity. This can be seen in the light of what was said earlier in the dichotomy parent/teenager. In many cases, the two individuals are still changing and making adjustments at their own personal level. To put it more simply, it is very difficult to save someone from drowning when one doesn't master the art of swimming oneself.

Therefore, the second great mistake that most parents make when confronted with an unmanageable teen is the following: they assume that the only problem comes from the youth but never consider their own behaviour and reactions. The focus must be directed on the parents because it is their choice of response and way of being which will be crucial for a good interaction with their teens. If the couple is stable and the two parents are in agreement with an adequate behaviour to have, things might go well; but if one parent is left alone and has to cope with the growing independence of the youngster, things could be more difficult, although they should work out very well if he or she has the right attitude. Equally, very united couples can have the wrong response and fail in building healthy communication with their teenagers.

Letting teenagers grow is sometimes challenging for both parents. I have observed that many fathers find it very difficult to admit that their daughter is in a relationship, and the same goes for mothers and their sons. Other parents are frightened by the "empty-nest syndrome" because they will find themselves alone, or just with their husband or wife after having been a family. A child is not a band aid for adults' wounds. They deserve to be blessed in their desire for independence. Adults have to deal with their own issues and not let these interfere with their relationship with their teens, or else this will undeniably result in tensions and conflicts. The parents who resent consciously or unconsciously their offspring leaving the home impede their natural evolution and create subsequent power struggles, dissatisfaction and long term frustration. Parents will allow them to grow by letting them go.

When there is a conflict between two people, even two adults, and that a mediator is called in to help thanks to his expertise, the solution will always stem from the awareness that changes have to be made on both sides. It is the combination between the two attitudes which poses a problem and both behaviours have to be analysed, put into question and subsequently altered.

If you look at the parents who incessantly complain about their teenagers, they very rarely, if not ever, question themselves. Let's take an example to illustrate this. Imagine a little child who is hospitalised because he or she has a broken leg. Without even giving it a second thought, the parents are going to slide into a behaviour focused on the wellbeing of the child. This happens very naturally. They are going to be empathic and actively helpful. The child will be surrounded by love, attention and gifts from family and friends; he or she will receive help from doctors and parents and will gradually walk again, encouraged by all the support. So much so that it is common practice for children who want more loving attention from their parents, to make out they are feeling unwell.

Identically, one has to provide adequate response to young-sters who behave badly. We have to realise that something in them is broken and we have to do all we can to help them. The key is not to focus on the disturbing behaviour but on its compatibility with our reaction to it. Just like a chess game, each move will have an effect on the next. I shall demonstrate, further on, easy ways of de-dramatis-ing objectionable teenage behaviour, such as foul speech, aggressiveness, indifference and so on.

Most well-intentioned parents fail in their attempt to com-municate with their teens because they don't change any-thing in their own mindset. An authoritarian parent who has always set very strict limits to his children will try to do the same when they get older and the result is very often disastrous. Moreover, as the teenager's behaviour is bound to get worse, the sanctions will very probably be reinforced. All this leads to failure and tension. I know a family in which the father was so authoritarian that his three children left home as soon as they could and subsequently cut all kind of relationship or contact with him. They all emigrated to far-away countries to make sure that the geographical space between their father and themselves was big enough, giving them the illusion that they were out of reach from his influence.

One has to understand that adolescence constitutes essen-tially a phase of self-government and of estrangement from old dependencies. On the cognitive level, it is about getting rid of old structures to experience new ones, on the affective level, it is about breaking from parents to engage with other people and creating new bonds, meaning a total personal restructuring moving away from parental identification. On the social level, the youth is looking for integration to social and economic life but not sieved through the family's control. Generally speaking, one can say that it is a period in which the adult identity is emerging, meaning that the adolescent is becoming more conscious of himself or herself and consequently more autonomous when it comes to making choices. The youth's childhood references are not satisfying anymore because he or she is looking for new sources of identification.

A common mistake adults make is thinking that the limits they had to give their children at an early age have to be applied in the same manner to teenagers. There is a simple reason why this is totally wrong. Thanks to Piaget, we know that teenagers start having a thinking ability, also called *abstract thinking* compared to children who have *concrete thinking*. Young children need limits because they are incapable of fixing them themselves. Moreover, teens need to experience the consequences of their own decisions and do not want to accept ready-made fix-its because this would imply that they are incapable of making their own mind about something.

Very young children have to be told not to go out on the road because at that age they are still is cognitively unable to realise the danger. Teenagers, however, don't have to be told not to hitchhike at two o'clock in the morning firstly because, ultimately, they know it is risky, and secondly because they have to make their own decisions and subsequently grow through the consequences. The parents can imply that it would be unadvisable to do so but must not impose their thoughts. As we shall see later, there are ways of getting the message over to them in a more effective way than just giving orders. Ideally the right decision should be handed over to the teen or, in other words, we have to show them that they can make the right decisions themselves.

This is precisely why the usual practice which is ultimately to set limits to the teenagers to control them is not a good solution. Obviously, youths must know what they can or cannot do, but if they don't have the freedom to experiment, the new limits merely imposed by the parents will never become owned and recognised as valid by them. To be able to be convinced of the rightfulness of limits, teenagers have to draw their own red line and this can only come from their own decisive mind and not imposed from anybody else. Parents must not let the youths do just anything but they must not push their guidance too far either. It is this balance that is so difficult to find.

My mother used to say: 'How annoying one cannot learn from others' experience, it would be such a gain of time!' That is not how it works. Experience is personal and cannot be taught.

DIFFERENT KINDS OF PARENTING

Françoise Dolto put in all in a nutshell when she said: 'You need great maturity to be capable of being a parent, because it implies being conscious that it is not a situation of power but a situation of duty and that we must not expect any kind of right in exchange.'

The subject of parenting has been covered by numerous theories and beliefs. In the 17th century, two philosophers independently wrote works that have been widely influential in child rearing. John Locke's 1693 book *Some Thoughts Concerning Education* is a well-known foundation for educational pedagogy. Locke highlights the importance of experiences to a child's development, and recommends developing their physical habits first. In 1762, the French philosopher Jean Jacques Rousseau published a volume on education, *Emile or, On Education*.

Locke proposes that early education should be derived less from books and more from a child's interaction with the world. His theory is basically that education makes the man: 'I think I may say that of all the men we meet with, nine parts of ten are what they are, good or evil, useful or not, by their education.' He advocates for an original *tabula rasa* theory of mind, but nevertheless did believe in innate talents and interests. For example, he advises parents to watch their children carefully to discover their aptitudes and to nurture their children's own interests rather than force them to participate in activities which they dislike. He also says that 'by treating children as rational creatures and recognizing their innate desire to grow in this propensity, parents guide their children towards reasoning abstractly and practicing reasonable actions later in life.' He also favours a degree of discipline and severity which should 'be relaxed as fast as their age.' Since the child longs to show independence of thought and takes pride in his or her liberty, granting confidence and encouraging reasonable discourse is the best method for a parent to have an effective and positive influence on the child. Once he has grown, his will then rule his actions and passions in the place of his parents. 'Since children naturally love liberty, desire to be treated rationally and are curious about the adult world,' it makes sense that 'earlier perhaps than we think they become sensitive to praise and need to be esteemed by their parents.'

Rousseau was influenced by Locke but his view is different in many ways. On the whole, Rousseau was more consistent with what would be called today "slow parenting" while

Locke was more for concerted cultivation on how to make the perfect gentlemen. Rousseau's famous quote is: 'Everything is good as it comes from the hands of the Maker of the world but degenerates once it gets into the hands of man.' Instead of an educated man being guided by societal norms, Rousseau desires for a child to have no other guide than his own reason by the time he is educated. Unlike Locke he does not rely on social expectations to train children. Rousseau contends that men can attain this freedom and independence of thought through naturalistic education. For Rousseau, when nature and society conflict with each other, one must decide between making a good man or making a good citizen, and he chooses the first option. However, when the child becomes an adolescent, things change:

> As the roaring of the waves precede the tempest, so the murmur of rising passions announces his tumultuous change; a suppressed excitement warns us of the approaching danger. A change of temper, frequent outbreaks of anger, a perpetual stirring of the mind, make the child almost ungovernable. He becomes deaf to the voice he used to obey; he is a lion in a fever; he distrusts his keeper and refuses to be controlled.

Let's shift from educational philosophies to parenting practices and styles. Parenting practices are specific behaviours while parenting styles represent broader patterns of parenting practices. Parenting style is the emotional climate in which parents raise their children. It is a psychological construct which represents standard strategies used in child rearing.

One of the main references for parenting styles was defined back in 1967 by Diana Baumrind, a famous clinical and developmental psychologist who focused on their classification known as "Baumrind's parenting typology", based on four basic traits that would define successful parenting: *responsive* versus *unresponsive* and *demanding* versus *undemanding.*

Being responsive refers to the extent to which parents are accepting and sensitive to the children's emotional needs and their basic developmental requirements. As to being demanding, Baumrind implies the degree to which parents control their children's behaviour or expect maturity from their part. Through her studies, Baumrind identified three initial parenting styles: authoritative parenting, authoritarian parenting and permissive parenting. In 1983, American psychologists Eleanor E. Maccoby and John A. Martin built upon these styles and placed them into two distinct categories: demanding and undemanding. They were thus able to define four parenting styles, adding the neglectful one._

Maccoby and Martin's Four Parenting Styles
Baumrind's Three Parenting Styles

	Demanding	**Undemanding**
Responsive	Authoritative	Permissive
Unresponsive	Authoritarian	Neglectful

Baumrind believed that parents should be neither punitive nor aloof, rather, they should develop rules for their children and be affectionate with them. Here are the main definitions that she gave.

Authoritative parenting is an approach which is centred on the child. The parents expect maturity from their children and encourage communication. They do understand that the children need to gain independence; however, they also set some limits to guide them. For Baumrind, '[the authoritative parent] encourages verbal give-and-take, shares with the child the reasoning behind her policy and solicits the child's objections when he refuses to conform.' In other words, the parent is both responsive and demanding.

Authoritarian parenting is much more restrictive. Children have to obey their parents without ever questioning them or getting any constructive feedback. Authoritarian parents use extreme means such as corporeal punishment, hard discipline and shouting. In Baumrind's words, '[such parents] value obedience as a virtue and favour punitive, forceful measures to curb self-will.' Unlike the authoritative parenting, demandingness is not counterbalanced by responsiveness.

Indulgent or *permissive parenting* (also called *non-directive, lenient* or *libertarian*) is a style in which parents are very involved with children but in a positive way, having little control or demands but still favouring communication. They are more like friends than parents. 'The permissive parent, according to Baumrind, attempts to behave in a non-punitive, acceptant and affirmative manner towards the child's impulses, desires and actions. She consults with him about policy decisions and gives explanations for family rules.'

Finally, *neglectful* or *uninvolved parenting* is when parents are distant and self-centred. They let their children get on by themselves and have no demands. There is no communication and no responsiveness. Such parents usually focus on their own lives at the expense of their children's; they are both physically and emotionally absent.

Based on these tendencies, I would like to simplify the matter greatly by pointing out three extreme parenting styles and suggesting one simple one to follow. I am purposely choosing a simple terminology.

The *bossy parent*, the detached parent and the *helicopter parent* and finally the one I think is the best, which would be the consultant parent or facilitator.

The *bossy parent* has all the bad sides of the *authoritarian parent* and wants to set the rules and keep control on his teen, giving him orders, demanding specific behaviour and having a power struggle the whole time.

The second would be the other extreme, the *detached parent* who hides away from confrontation and lets the teenager do whatever he wants without any sort of constructive communication mainly because he doesn't know how to handle adolescence. Such parents do not involve themselves in the education of their children.

The third one which is also excessive in a way, are the parents who would go under the definition of *helicopter parents*. An early 21st-century colloquial term for a parents who pays

extremely close attention to their children's experiences and problems and attempt to sweep all obstacles out of their path. These want the best for their children but go about it the wrong way. They constantly hover over their children and touch down whenever there is a crisis to solve, showing them their deep concern and reassuring them with the quick-fix that they will provide.

I must admit that I started out as a helicopter mother but realised that this seemingly caring approach does quite the opposite because it deprives the teenagers of their own capability of working things out. If their parents are constantly hovering over them, they will never learn how to defend themselves, how to get over difficulties, how to see and accept consequences and how to become independent adults.

The *helicopter parent* takes on the teen's responsibility by too much guidance at a time when gradual development of independence and self-sufficiency are essential for future success. It's up to the teen to own the problem and find a solution. If we fly in straight away to protect them, they will never achieve healthy independence and will not trust their own decisions. Modern communication technology has promoted this style by enabling parents to keep watch over their kids through cell phones, emails, online monitoring of academic grades and even tracking.

In conclusion being authoritative and bossy with threats, orders and lectures is destructive for the teens who will suffer on many levels: personality, self-concept and trust building. Constantly bossed around, they will have no way of thinking for themselves. The relationship will worsen with time.

Letting teens get on all alone without showing any care or any involvement will be similarly destructive, they will feel rejected and will lose all confidence.

Continual interference and immediate problem solving will take away their autonomy and decision making. The children will be helped but stifled at the same time.

The parent which is the best kind for me would be the *consultant parent*, a type which has been very well defined by Foster Cline and Jim Fay in *Parenting Teens with Love and Logic* (1992).One who never dictates or orders but advises, guides, understands, listens and most importantly adopts an adequate response in every situation. The consulting parents' concern for their children is omnipresent but doesn't always have to be blatantly visible. It is rather an implicit, in-depth interest. Such parents allow their teenagers to express themselves, to make mistakes, to find their own solutions, they never shout, give ultimata or threats. But they are as solid as a rock. Such parents would be more like therapists by letting the "patient" be, guiding the adolescent and ultimately wanting him or her to thrive. In order to build a balanced grown-up, they will talk to the teenager as they would to an adult and, more importantly, spend a lot of time listening. It will also guarantee mutual respect.

Besides, there is another category which is completely separate: toxic-parenting. This is naturally not a style but a result of mental disorders or addiction on the part of fathers, mothers and sometime of both at the same time. Children who are victims of this kind of treatment often need a very long time to be able to express their distress. They need to be helped professionally as well as protected against such terribly destructive abuse. Awareness of such crimes is making its way slowly but surely and many countries today offer hot lines for children who find the courage to speak out.

Susan Jane Broda Tamburi

INFLUENCE OF BIRTH ORDER

In the game that is played in family dynamics, every detail counts, and birth order can be one of them. How birth order could affect personality in teens is an interesting topic. Scientific research on the social phenomenon of birth order naturally leads to generalisations. One's own experience may somehow align with the findings or differ completely from the general data. Experts themselves disagree on the importance of birth order research. Nevertheless, the information is worth some thought. Here are some common birth order stereotypes:

Eldest children: high achievers, natural leaders, know-it-alls, rule-followers, who know how to be organised, punctual and responsible.

Middle children: perfectionists who can be adaptable, easy-going, social and independent, but also secretive and indecisive; to them, life may seem unfair.

Youngest children: risk-takers who can be self-centred, competitive and creative; they might also be outgoing, funny or spoilt, as well as easily bored and adventurous.

Only children: leaders who can be mature, demanding and dependable; there are nonetheless private, sensitive, self-centred or spoilt, but close to parents and well-educated.

Certain factors seem to modify these stereotypes, including the number of children in the family and their age gaps, their gender, their temperament, family illnesses, life changes, such as divorce, blended families, death, financial gains or losses and parents' own birth orders.

When asked to describe their teenage children, parents often reply: 'Oh, she's such a middle child,' or 'He's a typical first born!' But parents need to understand their teens' personalities and tendencies instead of blindly following stereotypes. Parents have to identify how the child feels according to birth order and help alleviate the stress. Parents should give extra attention to children who feel insecure when compared to their siblings, regardless of birth order. There are subtleties that have to be considered, If the oldest child is a girl for example and the second child a boy, both children may assume the traits of a first-born child. Also the birth order position of each parent could play a role.

Many parents have higher expectations for their oldest child. In some situations, the parents become excessively critical of their firstborn. Family psychologist, Dr Kevin Leman, and author of *Birth Order Book*: *Why You Are the Way You Are*, calls this the "critical-eyed" parent. He believes that a parent who relentlessly criticises the eldest child can dramatically alter the child's path to becoming a reliable, conscientious leader. Typically, when this occurs, the primogeniture no longer fits the firstborn paradigm, and the second child may occupy the space.

A 2005 study from researchers at Duke University, Johns Hopkins University and the University of Maryland confirms this theory. The study "Games Parents and Adolescents Play (…)" finds evidence that more severe discipline of older children discourages younger siblings from engaging in activities for which older ones were penalised. This same study also concludes that 'the possibility of such punishment deters oldest children from rebelling. Generally, the middle child is the opposite personality of the firstborn and different from the other siblings. Middle children are often the hardest to stereotype or describe.'

Very often, discipline relaxes with each child. By the time the youngest becomes a teenager, parents are more laid back and act less as disciplinarians. Studies show that birth order could affects career choices too. Firstborn and only children are more likely to pursue occupations that use their intellectual and cognitive skills. Cadets tend to pursue artistic and outdoor-related careers.

I think that ultimately birth order is not something to worry about but just something to keep in mind. It is important not to compare one child to another. Birth order is just one of the many factors that contribute to teens' unique position in a family although it appears to significantly impact some children's personalities. One has to see it as an influence rather than a scientific fact. No position in birth order is better than the other and every child is unique. The order in which one is born certainly doesn't give the full psychological portrait of an individual.

PERSONALITY COMBINATIONS

In the difficult alchemy of a good relationship between parents and children, there is an added element which can shuffle up the cards. Not only have we to take into account what is happening to the teenager on a physical and psychological level, we also have to consider different options of parenting modes. Let's add to that some degree of influence of birth order and the impact of general family dynamics. Finally, should we also throw into the equation the further complication of personality or character combination?

Some parents tell me that they can't deal with their teen-agers because of a personality or character clash. I have heard the following sentences so many times: 'I quit! my husband has to deal with our daughter, she and I are both headstrong, he manages her much better, he is so laid back.' or 'My wife is best at handling our son, she is much more understanding and patient.' Or even 'I can't manage girls, I just don't know how to deal with them, boys are easier.'

I would like to clarify this misunderstanding. First of all, one must differentiate character from personality. In the 1940s, mother-daughter team Isabel Briggs-Myers and Katharine Briggs worked to create a system to explain the differences in the ways people think, feel and behave. Based on the theory of psychological types proposed by the Swiss psychologist Carl Jung in 1921, the Myers-Briggs Type Indicator (MBTI) was first published in 1962. Then, with his 1978 book *Please Understand Me*, psychologist David Keirsey helped popularise and expand upon the framework. Today, millions of people have taken the test to determine their type. Without going in too much detail, here are some examples: Introverted, extroverted, sensing, intuitive, thinking, feeling, judging, perceiving. These are combined giving all possible personality types named with four-letter acronyms.

For instance, Extroverted, Sensing, Thinking, Judging would give ESTJ and would name you for example the Giver. Other nomenclatures are the Provider, the Idealist, the Performer and so on.

Personality refers to the combination of qualities, attitudes and behaviour that makes a person distinct from the other. It shows what you are on the outside. Traits of character on the contrary define the way a person is, not the way they think, feel or behave. You can be sensitive, aggressive, shy, etc. Character refers to a set of moral and mental qualities and beliefs that make a person differ from others. It indicates the traits of a person which are hidden from sight. While personality can be seen by others, character reveals what you are inside.

When things go wrong between two adults, for example two colleagues at work, one could put part of the blame on a difference of personality or character. When dealing with teenagers, this too has to be reconsidered. Although one's reactions to teenage behaviour does depend to a certain degree on what we are made of as individuals, it would be totally wrong to leave it at that. The maturity that is asked of us as adults is to know our own way of reacting and to adapt to the immediate circumstances of teenager turmoil that we are bound to face one day. The acknowledgement of one child's personality and character can be an added factor to take into account, but in my opinion, it is secondary at this stage. If you are a very emotional mother or a choleric father, you will have to work on yourself before being able to say that you have tried and failed to bridge the gap with your teen.

Evidently, it would be incredibly tedious to go through all the possible different combinations of the sixteen personality types or all of the various character traits and this is not of much interest for this matter. However, there are two elements that can be drawn out of these classifications which are of interest for my analysis.

Firstly, it is very important for us as parents to be able to define our own main character traits and to know how we react in some given circumstances because we are going to have to work on that, prior to getting involved in any kind of teenage management. It is the same self- analysis that has to be made when one becomes a teacher. So many of my acquaintances say 'I am not patient enough to be a teacher.' In that case people are free to choose another profession but parents can't just back out and say 'I'm not patient enough to deal with my eighteen-year old son or daughter.'

The second advantage of knowing the different psychological types and of being aware of general character traits is that it is a tremendously interesting test to do with your teenager at home or with students in class. Every time I experimented this both with my family or at work, the younger people were absolutely delighted to try to learn and know more about what kind of personality they had according the set of questions they had to answer. Let's have a look at what Sue Blair, director of *Personality Dynamics* and Nicky Gumbrell, language therapist, have to say about the experience of running a workshop on Personality Types.

It's a privilege to work with teenagers on Type. We have had the great pleasure of running workshops together for youths as part of their college leadership programme and we have enjoyed every moment. It's an exhilarating experience. Working with teens has its own special dynamic. At this age they are no longer cocooned, as are primary school kids, they have yet to stretch their wings and truly show their colours and fly. It's definitely an emergent phase. However, Type is innate, and to give these young people the opportunity to find out about who they are, and to know that it is OK to be that person, is an absolute privilege. Every teenager needs a "handle with care" label discretely tied to them as it's almost impossible to tell when they are having a fragile moment. If any of us could pick a time in our lives when we were at our most self-absorbed I would be willing to bet it would be in our mid-teens so what better time to put their minds to the taste of self discovery? – Sue Blair, "Type Works for Teens", published online at: www.personalitydynamics.co.nz/articles/type-works-for-teens/. Retrieved: 2018.)

EXCESSIVE PARENTAL INTERFERENCE

As we have just seen, when dealing with a person who is rebellious and in quest of his new identity at every level, parents must be extremely careful in adopting the right attitude.

We have seen all the transformations that the teenager is going through: first of all the physical transformations which calls for an unprecedented adaptation from the individual, then an identification of one's own image and a subsequent radical change in interior balance. Finally, the social status which becomes ambiguous, the individual not relating to a child anymore but not yet fully to an adult either, somewhere in between. This has to be not only understood but kept in mind constantly because parents are facing a person who still needs to be reassured and comforted as a child but at the same time, wants to be recognised and treated as an adult. He or she is simultaneously at a stage in life which demands many choices to be made like studies, first job, new lodgings, new relationships and so on.

In order to find a new identity, the youth has to be socially engaged and has to take new directions not only as far as personal opinions are concerned but also in his or her way of life. These options have to be adjusted and adapted to identity, personality and wishes. That is why the adolescent needs some kind of space to assess all the options. Henri Lehalle, a French developmental psychology professor, calls this a *psycho-social moratorium* (*moratoire psycho-social*). It is a period of time in which some decisions have to be put on hold so that the final ones have more chances to be successful. This is something that parents don't always see or want to see. It also means that the decisions adolescents take must sometimes be put in perspective because they might very well be only temporary. Teenagers think in extremes or sometimes on a whim and their decisions are subject to many changes.

During parents' sessions, I witnessed, over and over again, teenagers that were so clearly ill at ease with their parents who were imposing choices on them to which they didn't relate to at all. At these reunions, the conflict between parents and children was so palpable that I often felt very uncomfortable. There I was, expected to convince the youth to follow the wishes of his or her parents when all I wanted to do was to tell the parents that the problem was not with the child but with them. They were making choices for their child instead of withdrawing and trying to understand what was going on in their teenager's brain. I always try to use as much diplomacy as I can but I have always refused to this day to validate parents' opinions when it is so blatant that they are on the wrong track. Most of the teenagers having to choose a professional or training path are torn because they are trying to make the right choices but they are not quite sure if it's because they want to or because the decision will satisfy their parents. This identity crisis is automatically solved if the parents move out of the equation by letting their children make their own decisions and without influencing them directly or indirectly.

As Erikson said, the teenager feels the need to defend "a place of his own" against the excessive ideals of his parents. This is where the youth's choices have to be respected and given credit. He must not be forced into those that he has no will of pursuing. If the teenagers don't have any space for exploration and if they feel obliged to follow their parent's will, they will have serious identity problems later on in life. They will not know who they really are. As Erik Erikson pointed out, the search for identity marks an important step in adolescence. Adolescents may go through an identity crisis during which they struggle to understand themselves and decide on their future.

MARCIA'S FOUR IDENTITY STATUSES

The psychologist James E. Marcia, goes even further. He studied *vocation identity exploration* and *self-knowledge*. He assessed the process of vocation identity of the teenager on the threshold of adulthood (*vocation identity status assessment*). He based himself on two concepts already identified by Erikson: *crisis-exploration and commitment* and showed that further possibilities are given to the youth who is looking for his professional inclination.

Marcia devised the Identity Status Interview, a method of semi-structured interview for psychological identity research, which looks into a person's extent of "exploration" and "commitment" in various areas of their life. Evaluating the material provided in this interview by using a scoring manual, he described four possible identity statuses: *identity foreclosed*, *identity diffused*, *moratorium*, and *identity achieved*.

Marcia's four identity statuses

	Low commitment	**High commitment**
Low crisis exploration	Identity diffusion	Identity foreclosure
High crisis exploration	Identity moratorium	Identity achievement

Here are the definitions for each specific status.

Identity foreclosure happens when a person prematurely commits to values or roles that others prescribe. The teenager already knows what he or she wants to do later on, influenced by his or her social environment, parents' opinions, and close surroundings. The person has not engaged in any kind of research but follows a family scheme, willingly or under pressure, without having made any personal choice and without having assessed the correspondences with his or her own identity or desires. Marcia also mentions the case of *negative-identity*, that is when a youth purposely adopts an identity which blatantly goes against the one expected by his or her peer group, thus becoming a sort of alter ego of his or her parents. He also noticed that once an identity crisis has been experienced, it is no longer possible for the individual to return to the foreclosure status.

Identity diffusion occurs when a person lacks a clear sense of self but still hasn't explored issues related to identity development. Some adolescents seem to be overwhelmed by that task and are in a state of procrastination, social isolation and general withdrawal. Such youths may not have experienced an identity crisis while others show little interest in such matters. A common feature would be recurring indecision. Furthermore, such teens invest themselves so little into their future identity that they don't feel anxious about the situation. Eventually, after this long period of identity diffusion, the two most common outcomes seem to be either a delayed move to the *moratorium* status or a dangerous wandering which leads to a negative and self-destructive identity.

Identity moratorium is when a person is delaying commitment to an identity because he is experiencing high crisis exploration of various values and roles. More explicitly, such individuals are not sure about their identity and their commitments are either inexistent or not well-defined. However, they actively explore various possibilities in order to transform their unstable situation into something predictable and secure. Such people are often anxious about the situation, but on the other hand, they know they need time and experience to reach a satisfactory identity. This status, which used to be frowned upon in the past, is nowadays considered a constructive stage in life, which can take the form of multiple internships, sabbatical years, volunteering and so on.

Identity achievement exists when a person considers alternative possibilities (high crisis exploration) and commits to a certain identity and path in life (high commitment). Marcia states that: 'a likely progression would be from diffusion through moratorium to identity achievement.' This status shows that the teenager has gone through a process of active exploration and has found his own personal identity. It is a positive realisation which is the guarantee of personal blossoming and equilibrium.

Identity shifts means that the last stage of identity achievement does not exclude a change in orientation later on. Transitions are often inspired by various life changing events such as job loss, divorce, death of a loved one, change in socio-economic conditions, etc. It can lead to what Marcia calls the MAMA Circle: Moratorium –Achievement – Moratorium – Achievement. As far as professional choices are concerned, this circle means that a person who has found a job which corresponds to his inner identity could very well want to change direction after a few years of professional engagement by redirecting his or her activity. This period of reconstruction can also be motivated by a desire for further professional training, self-improvement, promotion, added interests or social progression.

Let's take the example of a young girl who has chosen the job of social assistant, which corresponds to her will and desire of helping others. After a few years, she could very well want to push forward her commitment and follow a course in nursing. Thus choices made in teenage-hood can very well be pursued later on in life although slightly redirected.

Whatever the reason when disequilibrium occurs, a period of reconstruction begins. During the reconstruction the person may regress to an earlier identity status but at some stage the old constructs are replaced with new ones which correspond more widely to the person's identity. The new construction is broader because it includes new life experiences and commitments.

If we apply Marcia's theories to everyday life, it confirms that we have to let our youths go through their experiences and trust them in doing so. This also means that we have to accept their mistakes, changes in orientation and hesitations. I am always appalled to see that we expect children at a very early age to know exactly what they want to do later on and to project themselves into a professional future when they are hardly able to cope with who they are. Too many parents ask of their children to follow a straight road in a world that is so complex and winding. Let's keep in mind that the true richness of adolescence is to have the impression of being at a crossroads where any choice is still possible. The young individual is at a threshold of his life. Although frightening, this is a magical moment. As mentioned earlier, responsibility cannot be taught, it must come from within. The best parents can do, is to offer opportunities to their teens to become responsible and not order them to do what they think would be labelled as responsible. Parents have to give their teens the chance to feel independent and allow them to feel in control handing back their feelings to them.

The constant preoccupation of giving a frame within which an adolescent can move and of directing him or her on a future professional track is, in many cases if not all, counterproductive. The temporary inactivity of teenagers must not always be associated with procrastination, lethargy or idleness. Too many parents fear that their children are going to step out of the educational highway and wander in unknown land. Much too often, parents apprehend some imaginary lurking delinquency in their teenager's laid-back behaviour. The way parents manage these fears will very often determine the outcome.

To illustrate what I mean, I like to use the image of a cat falling from some reasonable height. During the fall, the cat will rotate progressively, find its balance and finally land back on its feet. If one had interfered while the animal was falling, trying to catch it or trying to reduce the speed of the fall, one might well have gone against the laws of gravity and the cat could have hurt itself. The same goes with our teenagers, let's try to hold back on incessant intervention and let's give nature a chance. Let's trust them instead of imposing our thoughts on them. In both cases, that of the animal and the teenager, our role is to observe from our standpoint and hold our breath.

3

THE RIGHT ATTITUDE

LIMITS TO DISCIPLINE

There are a lot of things parents can do to help and we shall go through them one by one. Let's go back to the notion of discipline. According to me it is from this attitude that most problems arise. We are constantly reminded that the basis of all good education is setting limits and boundaries. Even though it is reassuring for children to know how far they can go, I believe, as mentioned previously, that this notion has to be reconsidered drastically when dealing with teenagers.

The usual reaction of parents facing teenager's dysfunction is to automatically re-enforce discipline and fix stricter rules. Such parents are invariably disappointed. Notwithstanding, they continue on the wrong path, oblivious of the fact that more discipline means more trouble.

So the person who has to change his behaviour in the conflict is the parent. We have to put our way of talking or reacting into question. We are the ones who have to make the effort. Some parents might be shocked by my approach because it goes against the grain of the pyramidal structure of parent giving orders and children obeying. However, the parents who dare try to change this structure for a short period of time are all unanimous in saying that things seem to cool down miraculously. Being stuck in a rut of wanting to overpower unruly teens leads nowhere.

The key to the problem is acknowledging that the adolescent is moving towards independence therefore he should not find himself in a situation of blind or forced obedience. We as parents have to understand that our reign is over. If we want our children to become adults we have to stop dominating them, adapting our role from authoritarian parent to understanding coach. Sometimes it goes even further and we must become witnesses of what is going on. We have to give the youths the tools to become independent and give them space to develop their new identity. We have to accept their egocentricity which is so characteristic of this stage of their development.

The equation is simple, we have two people, one who wants to become autonomous and the other who finds it very difficult to lose his grip on what is going on. Parents have to start letting go. This does not mean showing no interest or involvement in what the teenager is doing but it means observing from a distance what has to be done naturally and trying to hold back any behaviour that would put the whole operation in jeopardy. Much too often, parents feel that they are losing something in the process, losing control, losing the love of their children, losing an imaginary battle. On the contrary, parents will gain a lot in adopting this way of being, first of all they will maximise the chances of their children of becoming balanced adults, they will gain respect, real inbuilt respect not the artificial one that is born from fear.

THE PUNCHING-BALL APPROACH

All the observations made above point to one direction: putting into parenthesis the fears, needs, worries of the parents and focusing the light on the adolescent. Parents who accept being a punching ball will very quickly realise that the difficult period they are going through will be over very soon. Although during this period the parents will seem to have the second role, they are in fact going to perform the act of a lifetime. It is as if to enable the other one to grow and thrive, one has to back off for some time.

Let's imagine that a teenager went out until 3 or 4 o'clock in the morning and is sprawled on the sofa because he was too tired to reach his room. He has probably come home much later that the parents asked him to and has probably drunk a little more than they allowed him to. The next morning there are two options for the parents. Either they bully their child, waking him up, telling him off, starting an argument or they cover him with a blanket, close the door and let him sleep it out.

It is the second option that somehow represents the behaviour that I am suggesting and that I have named the *punching-ball approach*.

For a short period of time, parents have to accept being the one who will take the blows, who will feel frustration and sometimes even anger. One has to allow teenagers to try out provocation, one has to give them the space to rebel, one has to accept what is normally inadmissible, to be able to move on to something else. The more one goes against a teenager who wants to affirm himself, the longer the conflict will last. Parents who accept to yield will find the right path very quickly and the pre-existing relationship will reappear miraculously. Let's not forget, that what the adolescent is going through is only temporary. Parents have to buckle up and hold on. It is undeniably a rollercoaster. If we ask of our teenagers to become mature shouldn't we as adults show signs of maturity too?

UNWAVERING LOVE AND SUPPORT

Paradoxically, the adolescent who seems to be refusing our affection is in fact in deep need of it. The thin and intricate borderline between childhood and adulthood has to be given round the clock attention. Even if the teenagers criticise their parents and don't want anything to do with them, these have to prove again and again that whatever happens, they will always be supportive and present. The adolescent is like a young animal who wants to get further away from its parents to start the process of autonomy but who runs back to them in case of danger until the moment when it will cope with danger itself.

Parental presence must be unconditional and constant. Instead of finding endless reproaches concerning their behaviour, parents ought to spend more energy reassuring them about their support in case of trouble. The parents who give their children ultimata all the time make a great mistake. Sentences such as 'If you go on like this, you will have to leave home' or 'This is the last time I accept this behaviour' are destructive, sterile and alienating.

Showing our teens that we understand, love and support them is paramount. Too often parents are overwhelmed by the behaviour of their children and do not have time to express their love, which seems to be rejected like all the rest. Not only must we, as parents show that we shall always be there to defend and protect our children, but we have to express and formulate the love we have for them verbally.

One day I saw some graffiti on a school wall. The following message, painted in huge red letters was in front of me: 'MY FATHER IS ALWAYS YELLING AT ME, HE NEVER TELLS ME HE LOVES ME.' I was so shattered by this sentence that I was speechless for a few minutes. Having had an extremely loving father made this sentence sound even more shocking to me. Later on, I learnt that it was a young girl of eighteen from a neighbouring school who had expressed her distress the only way she could.

Once again, this shows that teenagers still have one foot in childhood and are in constant balance between the need of being autonomous and the need of recognition and being loved. Autonomy does not mean cutting the existing affective links with parents, it means creating others with a boyfriend or a girlfriend or just friends but with the unfailing security that parental love is as strong and long lasting as a rock. Teenagers don't need to be cuddled and kissed all the time but they absolutely need to know that their parents love them more than anything. This is the concrete foundation on which they will be able to build their own personal relationships with others.

SYMPATHY, EMPATHY AND COMPASSION

There is a difference between sympathy and empathy and the thinness of distinction between the two is worth analysing. Both words are used similarly and they are often interchanged but they differ in their emotional meaning.

Sympathy and empathy share a common root, the Greek noun *pathos* meaning feelings, emotion, or passion. Sympathy comes from *sympathes*, having common feeling. For example a teenager can sympathise with another one because he is going through the same fears or worries. Empathy (*empatheia*: "in-feeling") goes much further, it is not only an identification but also connotes an awareness of one's separateness from the observed. One of the most difficult tasks for a human being is reflective commitment to another's problem while maintaining his own identity. Empathy is an intellectual insight into another's emotional state without actually sharing it.

Applied to my analysis, parents are empathic when they understand what their teenager is going through although they are not experiencing the pain or the trauma themselves. Empathy is what is needed in the parent/teenager relationship. The parents imagine how the youth might feel based on what they know about him or her. Sympathy is not enough. Compassion takes things one step further. Compassion comes from the Latin (*cum patior* or "I suffer with"). It is a sympathetic feeling of pity coupled with the desire to alleviate pain, a willingness to relieve the suffering of others by doing something about it.

The Dalai Lama said in *The Art of Happiness* (1998): 'If you want others to be happy practice compassion. If you want to be happy, practice compassion.'

Empathy and compassion have to be constant during the conflictual period between teenagers and adults. Parents have to assess cognitively what is going on in their teenager, accept it, and do whatever possible to help without falling into the trap of solving problems for them by helping them solve their own.

THE NOTION OF PROJECT

When a youth gives signs he is going through a very difficult period, it is important in my view, to insist more on the future than on the present. This trick takes the pressure away from the "here and now" and projects the teenager in a future that can be presented as more reassuring. Mentioning what is going to happen in several months sends out a reassuring message. Even if the future is still uncertain, it is very constructive to slip some positive predictions into the conversation now and again, to show that a more pleasant period is close at hand.

I shall take the example of a student of mine who was following a commercial training, a choice that he had made against his parents will. Therefore, he was never totally self-confident. He seemed fragile, hesitant and very often self-critical. On the one hand he was eager to carry on in his professional choice but on the other hand, he was inhibited because of his parents' disapproval. When talking to him, I often referred to his future profession showing him that his graduation was a sure thing as far as I was concerned. I noticed that he was fuelled by the fact that I was showing trust in him and that I was implicitly validating his choice. Little by little he became more confident and looked less worried. He finally managed to get through his final exams and was successful in finding a very good job in a sector which corresponded to his interest and ambition.

It is not about giving young people the illusion that they will succeed in anything they do, it is about reassuring them that their choices might well be the right ones. We shall see further on, that in some cases, some choices teenagers make are not good ones in the end, but making mistakes, changing direction and adjusting is exactly what adolescence is all about. Taking time in discovering what is right for you is not a waste of time it is quality time.

POSITIVE REINFORCEMENT

One has to show children not only that they are loved and supported but also encouraged. It is in the United States that I found this positive attitude omnipresent and so determining for teenagers' development. The schools that I visited all had this constructive optimistic outlook. Sentences like: 'Making mistakes show that you are learning' are always very motivating.

Praising and congratulating are ways of reinforcing the adolescent's image of himself and a way of building his self-confidence. When teachers or educators say: 'Well done,' it gives young people tools to improve their achievements and push their limits. It is the same encouragement that former president Obama expressed in his famous speech when he said 'Yes we can.' It's in a way, mind over matter. To convince oneself that one can succeed is already half of the job done. It is also from the former president the message that everyone, even the Afro-Americans and all the minorities who feel oppressed, in one way or another, can reach their goals.

The Anglo-Saxon way of encouraging young people is often missing in countries where I have taught, such as France and Switzerland. Many times, the focus is put on what the student does wrong instead of what he is does right. Taking away marks for mistakes instead of giving points for achieved tasks. Overall achievement should count more. Things are changing in this respect, but at a very slow pace in my opinion.

My experience during a Master's degree exam years ago has stayed in my mind ever since. At first I was a little nervous because although I knew my subject well, which was *Beowulf,* I was not one hundred per cent certain of my understanding of Old English language. I knew that in the first part of the exam, I was going to be tested on the syntax itself and only in the second part would I have to develop a thorough thematic analysis. My American teacher felt my uneasiness and said to me 'I am here because I am interested in what you know, not what you don't, feel free to show me everything you have learnt and want to share.' This sentence set me free immediately and I started my linguistic and thematic analysis with so much confidence that nothing could have stopped me. I spoke for about twenty minutes without any pause. As my subject was *Language in Beowulf,* I wanted to show that at the end of the story, when Beowulf had been killed, the silence that prevailed in the castle was incredibly haunting and eerie and to illustrate that feeling I stopped speaking for one full minute for the teacher to experience sudden silence. I must have managed to communicate what I wanted to him because after my performance, he got up, shook my hand and thanked me. One week later I got the news that I had been given maximum grade and that he had asked me to be his assistant in the English Linguistic department that was going to open the following year.

I always keep in mind that magical moment when my students are passing an oral test. I always try to say something that will free their speech and make them feel confident. So many of my students say to me, even before their exam begins 'You will see, I am no good at oral tests.' Giving the students back their confidence is a guarantee of a better grade. If we imply to students that they can handle a situation or even excel at it, they will. We have to send messages to teenagers that they are able to think for themselves and achieve good things, little by little building their self-concept. They will not only learn to like themselves but will improve constantly.

What goes for oral exams also goes for teenagers who are shy, insecure or unsure about their future. So many of them think that they are not going to make it, not going to be performing adults, not going to land a good job, not going to be worthy of a relationship and so on. Parents have to change their discourse, they have to stop nagging at their teenagers and start encouraging and supporting them.

This self-trust will come naturally to a person who has received sufficient positive reinforcement. When we insinuate youngsters can deal with a situation, they succeed. When we imply that they are not capable of doing something, they will perform badly. This is the unconscious reasoning that they make: 'I don't become what you think I can become, I don't become what I think I can become, but I become what I think you think I can become.'

How to speak to teenagers is an issue that American broadcasting even includes in its television advertisements. At a frequency of about thirty times a day, viewers can watch a father trying to find the right way to communicate with his son, not knowing which one is best. In the one minute advert, you see the father oscillate between being cross, authoritarian, diplomatic and finally totally confused in front of his teenager who looks at him as if he were a total alien. The 24/24 hotline claims to help parents to find the right tone; they also have a website one can go to.

THE CONCEPT OF *CARE*

The basic meaning of the word *Care* is associated with the origins of the word, which are found in the Middle High German word *kar* and more remotely in the Common Teutonic word *caru*, meaning "trouble" or "grief" (Simpson and Weiner, 1989, pp. 893–894). Correspondingly, the primary meaning of the word "care" is anxiety, anguish, or mental suffering. A second meaning of "care" is a basic concern for people, ideas, institutions, and the like. The idea that something matters to the one who is concerned. Two other meanings of care, sometimes in conflict, are found at a more practical level. One is a solicitous, responsible attention to tasks, taking care of the needs of people and one's own responsibilities ; and the other is caring about, having a regard for, or showing attentive care for a person, for his or her growth, and so forth. In a sense, all the meanings of "care" share to some extent one common basic element: one can scarcely be said to care about someone or something if one is not at least prepared to worry about him, her, or it.

Care is the very word that has found its place in Anglo-Saxon field of educational psychology. The American philosopher Milton Mayeroff was one of the first to work on this concept. In his book *On Caring* (1971), he provides a detailed description and explanation of the experiences of caring and being cared for. Although he drew on several major themes from the history of the notion, he took the idea of care in a new direction.

All the theorists agree that *care* is about dependence and vulnerability. The original idea implies that individuals cannot be one hundred per cent autonomous. They need to establish relationships with others to satisfy their biological and psychological needs. If this dependence is particularly visible in infancy, childhood, old age or sickness, it is nevertheless present during our whole life. To care for another, according to Mayeroff, is to help the other grow ; for example, the basic caring stance of a parent is to respect the child as striving to grow in his or her own right. Helping other persons to grow also entails encouraging and assisting them to care for something or someone other than themselves, as well as for themselves.

In his view, caring entails devotion, trust, patience, humility, honesty, knowing the other, hope and courage. Knowledge, for instance, means being able to sense "from inside" what the other person experiences and requires to be able to grow. Devotion, which gives substance and a particular character to caring for a particular person, involves being "there" for the other courageously and with consistency. But caring does not mean "being with" the other constantly. Phases of caring and of relative detachment should alternate.

In Mayeroff's vision, moral values are inherent in the process of caring and growth. When cared for, one grows by becoming more self-determining and by choosing one's own values and ideals grounded in one's own experience, instead of simply conforming. Caring involves trusting the other to grow in his or her own time and way. One who "cares" too much is not showing excessive care for the other but rather a lack of trust in the other's potential and capacity of growing.

Nel Noddings, American feminist and philosopher specialised in education, followed up on this notion of *care*. She says that *care* is a asymmetric relationship in which a care-giver is sensitive to the needs of a recipient and tries to respond to him or her. There is a movement towards the other and towards the other's interests. For Noddings, the best example of this relationship is between mother and child, and that is why, at the beginning, her theory was labelled as feminine. However, the relationship she describes is valid for all human relationships. Noddings goes even further, extending her findings to other kinds of relationships: teacher/student, trainer/trainee, doctor/patient. This is what Mayeroff calls this human exchange devotion or altruism.

In her study *The Challenge to Care in Schools. An Alternative Approach to Education* (1992) and even more so in her second edition (2005), Noddings develops this idea. She shows that at school students have different strengths and that these different capabilities should be cultivated in an environment of caring, not competition. She suggests that teachers should make the responsiveness characteristic of caring more basic than mere accountability. The concept of "caregiving" coming from teachers gives teenagers emotional security. The first step is to first develop a trusting relationship with the students by listening to them and understanding their claims. I find that the notion of *care* is exactly the right attitude to have when dealing with adolescents in general, not only in the classroom.

4

HANDLING UNACCEPTABLE BEHAVIOUR

SYSTEMATIC CONTRADICTION

There are some typical behaviour patterns that teenagers will have and that we, as parents, have to learn how to cope with efficiently. Let's keep in mind, that adolescence is a moment of reflexive orientation and self-centring. It is also a period of disengagement from the family. Non-conformism or rebellion, call it what you will. By changing their overall status wanting to become autonomous, teenagers are going to try to find a new place in their social environment and this is going to change the way others look at them. At this stage it is as though language is no longer a valid or trustworthy means of communication and the teens are going to use other ways of transmission like contradiction, provocation, silence, withdrawal or even risky behaviour.

Although parents rightfully resent systematic contradiction from their children, they have to get used to the fact that most of their decisions, suggestions thoughts or opinions are going to be contested and opposed for some time. It would be illogical for teenagers, who are going through a process of independence, to accept blindly what comes from their parents. It would be a kind of regression. They absolutely need to have their own opinion on everything, and even if sometimes they actually agree with their parents, they will very seldom confess it. Adults must then prove that they have the maturity to accept all this criticism for what it is worth.

The position of a young child of seven or eight who just believes without any question all that parents say or that of a teenager who is in systematic opposition to all they put forward are both equally extreme. In the first case the child is accepting things not knowing whether they could be wrong, and in the second one, the teenager is refusing things that are probably right.

It is sometimes very amusing to see that teenagers will disagree with what their parents say even if the idea doesn't seem that bad to them. It is as though for a suggestion to be validated, it has to emanate from their own brain or line of thought. Just accepting whatever opinion comes from their genitors is not feasible. Either your teenager will contradict you or remain silent. Very rarely will he or she agree wholeheartedly. Nevertheess, it is common knowledge that your views and values will very probably be shared by your children later on in life. If a children have grown up in a household with strong ethical values, there is a good chance that they will become caring adults even though they will contest some of these notions during adolescence. Just like a boomerang, if good examples are set from the start, they will come back in some shape or form later on. Other parents feel that their teenager's contradictory attitude is related to a lack of love. They are obviously misinterpreting the signs. It is not because your children love you that they have to adhere to all the values your set. In other words, if they don't agree with you that does not imply that they don't have any affection for you. They need to have their own opinion. Likewise, some decisions made by teenagers hurt their parents without reason. I have a friend who is always nervous around the middle of December because she fears that her three sons might not spend Christmas with her and her husband, although all three of them are in a relationship and are over nineteen! Teenagers are in quest of inclusion but at the same time, they want to be free. They will do things that seem hostile to the family but which are in reality just normal.

The worst attitude parents can have is to try to impose their point of view or to demand something of teenagers. During this fragile period, the roles have to inverse themselves. Our suggestions and advice will go nowhere. The archaic pyramidal structure of parents giving orders and children obeying must be destroyed. Donald Winnicott, a famous English paediatrician and psychoanalyst, had already understood that a teenager cannot accept solutions that are just imposed on him or her from the outside. The youth will refuse any kit or quick-fix that comes from parents who want to show they know better. As Winnicott says, "The teenager does not want to be understood" at this stage because that would mean that the solution could not come from within. Again, it is all about making one's own decisions.

WITHDRAWAL AND ANTISOCIAL BEHAVIOUR

This behaviour is very frequent in teenagers who feel the need of isolating themselves. I have renamed this, the *three door syndrome*. The teenager avoids any direct communication, speaks less and regularly withdraws moodily from any contact. The *three door syndrome* is when the youth comes home, bangs the front door, then goes to the fridge, gets something out of there for immediate consumption and shuts it violently, and then goes to his or her room and bangs that door too. As queer as this behaviour may seem and as bewildered it can make parents feel, it has to be considered as more or less predictable. At that precise moment, it is often all the youths are capable of doing. They need isolation from the family group and want to be left alone. Therefore, it would be counterproductive to take teenagers up on their seemingly rude attitude. Just as it is useless to ask them to apologise. The best way would be trying to see the comical side of this and to tolerate this anti-social behaviour on the grounds that it is just temporary. Addressing the problem on the spot would be a mistake.

I remember the case of parents who insisted that their three teenagers would wait for their father to come home around 9 pm every evening to have dinner all together and to be able to communicate, talking about each other's day. This rigid structure did not hold long and communication within the family worsened as time went on. What seems right in theory is not always advisable in reality. With teenagers, one has to engage in communication when the moment is right, and that moment has to come from them, for it to be constructive. Communication *per se* is of no use if it is going to create tensions. The best barometer is to see how the teenager behaves after the exchange. If he or she is angry or remains silent again, that means that communication has failed, and the next opportunity might be a long way away.

Personally I have had extremely constructive exchanges with my teens when I expected it the least. At the most surprising moments, they would come to me and start talking about crucial emotions or issues they wanted to share. The challenge is precisely to catch those moments when they occur. We have to do our best to make ourselves available because very often, important information is going to be presented to us at that precise instant. Installing a predetermined, definite, regular moment for communication goes against the chaotic rhythm the adolescents are experiencing. They need to be willingly talkative and this will not happen if the scheduling of the conversation is set arbitrarily by anybody than themselves.

RISKY AND ERRATIC BEHAVIOUR

Teenagers will also probably start adopting dangerous, excessive behaviour. We now know that these are made possible by the still incomplete structure of part of their brain. The limbic system triggers off the impression of the feeling-good sensation, when taking risks. The use of drugs, smoking or a sudden drive for getting a crazy tattoo or doing something dangerous is more than frequent. The response has to be carefully thought out because if the parents react too strongly it might have the opposite effect. Here again, understanding and guidance is needed instead of blind authority. Unconsciously all these behaviours are aimed at fighting authority, so if more control is piled on, the reaction could be extremely negative.

More often than not, the fact of taking up smoking or light drugs will subside naturally because the teenager just wants to try something new and daring. Building a strong self-concept is the most important thing parents can do so that when the teen reaches the age of temptation, there is a good chance he or she will not engage in risky behaviour for long.

One good solution to combat risky behaviour could be to encourage teenagers to take up sports that do involve some kind of risk, channelled by a coach, for example hang gliding or rafting. The teenagers will be proud of doing something which boosts their adrenaline, and will be satisfied with their parents showing them some trust.

Neutralising teen erratic behaviour is easy if you remember that teenagers think in extremes. One day they are up, the next they are down. Time is your best ally. When you feel you are not going to be able to stay calm, leave the room, find an excuse, let the tension subside by letting go of immediacy. Troubleshooting doesn't have to be immediate. When there is a misunderstanding or when the situation seems irrational, things don't have to be solved on the spot. Time is needed to see things in context. Very often the following day, the teenager will have forgotten the urgency of a claim or a decision. Take time in finding the solution and putting things into perspective or even better, take time in waiting for the teenager to find a solution or to work out the consequences by himself.

I remember a funny episode that happened when I was in Poland one summer. My mother-in-law was one of the most popular women in the village mostly inhabited by widowed women who helped each other on a daily basis for everything from cooking, shopping, gardening, to childcare. She used to help all her family with the bringing up of toddlers (including mine when she came over to Switzerland) but also offered her services willingly to her neighbours' and friends' children, acting as a nanny and babysitter. Although she was not always pedagogical in all her approaches when dealing with young children, surprisingly enough, she knew exactly how to deal with one of her friends' teenage daughter who was going through a period of deep crisis. Added to the fact of being eighteen, the young girl had to cope with being pregnant and living with her unemployed husband to be in her parent's home, with an alcoholic father. My mother-in-law was invited on a daily basis to have morning coffee in that household but always phoned before crossing the street enquiring *'Anita humory ma dzisiaj?'* meaning 'Is Anita in a bad mood today?' If the answer was *'Tak'* meaning 'Yes' she would simply not go to visit them until tea time! I found this instinctive reaction full of philosophical wisdom. She knew that confrontation with a female teenager let loose was going to be a losing battle and that only time would smooth things out. To ensure that she would spend a relaxing moment with her friend, she thus alternated her visits from coffee time to tea time according to Anita's daily disposition. Funnily enough the young girl often turned to my mother in law for advice on a regular basis and later on even trusted her to look after her little baby boy!

MISJUDGMENTS AND LIES

Misjudgement is by far the most dangerous teenage flaw in my opinion. Indeed, as teenagers want to make their own decisions and simultaneously not being mature enough for taking the right ones, we as parents experience some frightening moments. From setting off hitch-hiking across south America alone or mingling with non-recommendable people, the list is a long one and each family has its own share of crazy and erratic decisions thrown at them. Even if we now understand that teenagers don't think like adults, one often has to find a hasty solution when faced with these unexpected challenges.

Constructive dialogue is then needed, even if any kind of dialogue is not usually what teenagers like at this point. One has to make them realise for themselves that their decisions could be, if not changed, at least improved in a way. Here again any direct criticism is going to backfire. Constructive questioning about the decision or calling in a neutral outsider may help. For example, call in one of your teenager's friends to help him or her see things differently. Ultimately the teenager will have to own his decision and go through the consequences. Personally I often asked my more mature child to counsel the younger one and more often than not it worked miracles.

Some parents might think that what I am suggesting is shocking in a way. Not only do I advocate giving up any kind of authoritarian attitude, or any equal to equal attitude as it were but I am encouraging the parent to put himself into a situation of temporary submission. Instead of being the usual standard parent who is in charge, one has to become an anti-parent in a way. The idea is to give our teenagers some kind of authority over us knowing that it is the only way to move on, so that there is no power struggle, no loser but just two winners: the teen and the parent.

Although this suggestion seems out of the ordinary, it is a guarantee of success and will restore a healthy relationship when the teenage period is over. It is as though you gave over authority and decision making to your teenager until he or she gets to the age when everything will be done naturally in mutual understanding and consent.

I would like to illustrate this once again: it is exactly like when you are sitting in the car next to your teenager who is learning how to drive. More than once, you will feel afraid, nervous, worried but you know that this mustn't show.

Then, miraculously, one day, you will feel so comfortable and at ease, that you may even doze off on a long journey knowing that your kid is in control of the road, of the traffic and, ultimately, of your life. You will have shifted from worrying to trusting.

The message that one has to give teenagers is that we trust them and this is what they are desperately seeking without really being able to express it. Trusting your teenagers is the greatest gift you can give them. It means that you are making their journey to independence smoother, it also means that you are actively building stronger human beings. The only notion that has to be present at all times apart from total trust is unconditional love. Showing that our teens will be loved and supported all along the way is crucial. This is the best way to create a positive outcome and to secure a healthy and lasting quality relationship.

As children enter adolescence they begin to act more evasively to get more room to grow, and they are more and more prone to lying both by commission, telling a deliberate falsehood or by omission not voluntarily disclosing all that parents need to know. Parents will also be confronted by the fact that their teenagers will sometimes tell lies either to cover up something they did wrong and are mature enough to realise how wrong it was, or to delay any kind of confrontation or even to invent part of their personality that has not yet reached its full construction. Lying always has to be de-dramatised and put into context. As annoying, confusing and even hurtful as being lied to is, it is actually part of a child's normal development. In fact, some researchers think that a child's first lie is a positive milestone in mental growth. Although it is not to be encouraged, it is something to expect in teenage parenting. The most frequent lies teenagers tell are about drinking, drugs and fear of punishment. At times this will be calculated and elaborate, at others, instinctive and awkward. Sometimes they think they are protecting their parents because deep down they do value their opinion and are in need of their approval. Not wanting to let parents down can be another motivation for lying.

Lies can also be directed towards people other than parents when the teen wants to validate an identity that he doesn't have. To show off or to look better than he is in reality. This should subside with time. Finally, lying can be a cry for attention.

The reaction to all kinds of lying is to adopt an attitude which is in no way questioning or lecturing. The more you interrogate your teens, the more they will get defensive and secretive. Instead of accusing them of not revealing the truth, it is more constructive to understand why they disguise reality and build something positive around that. Acknowledging a lie, whether inconsequential or not without making them feel bad about it will minimise the whole process. Not making a big deal of it will have as a consequence that next time the teenager might not even bother.

The important thing here is to listen to what is being said, even to silences or hesitations. One has to try to extrapolate from what is said or hidden. Being ready to hear the truth means also hearing things that could be shocking. Birth control, early pregnancy, bad relationships, parents have the difficult task of being prepared to listen without being judgemental. Little by little the teens will suffer more about lying to their parents because they will feel lonely in their untruths. As they move forward, trusting your reaction and guidance, they will also move away from their early lying strategy which will in time destroys itself.

5

TEENAGERS FACING OTHER ISSUES

ADOPTED TEENAGERS

I have many friends who have adopted children and most of them have a hard time when the child becomes a teenager. To understand what is at stake, one has to go through some basic knowledge about adoption itself. Many people believe that if a child has suffered an upbringing that was lacking in love and support, he or she will be able to settle and flourish with a new family that provides what is needed. However, while stability and acceptance help to give a foundation in which a child can grow and find a healthy state of being, these qualities make up only one part of what is required.

Donald Winnicott referred to earlier, is one of the biggest references for this topic. His second wife, Clare Britton, was a psychiatric social worker and he learnt a lot from her experience working with disturbed children who had been evacuated during World War II. She examined the difficulties faced by children who were either orphans or displaced trying to adapt to a new home.

Winnicott who was strongly influenced by the two psychiatrists Sigmund Freud and Melanie Klein, notes in his paper entitled *Hate in the Countertransference*: 'It is notoriously inadequate to take an adopted child into one's home and love him.' Although this sentence can be shocking, let's see what he meant by this. If fact the parents must be able to take the adopted child into their home and be able to tolerate hating him. Winnicott states that a child can believe he or she is loved only after being hated, he stresses that the role that 'tolerance of hate' plays in healing cannot be underestimated. He explains that when a child has been deprived of proper parental nurturing, and is then granted a chance of this in a healthy family environment, such as with an adoptive or foster family, the child begins to develop unconscious hope. But fear is associated with this hope. When a child has been devastatingly disappointed in the past with even basic emotional or physical needs unsatisfied, defences arise. These are unconscious forces that protect the child against the hope that may lead to disappointment. In Winnicott's view, the child must be allowed to express that hatred and the parent must be able to tolerate both the child's and their own hatred as well. There are many ways for a child to express that he or she is indeed not worthy of being loved. This worthlessness is the message that was imported by earlier negative parenting.

When they reach adolescence, adoptive children have an added burden to deal with. They have to go through the gruelling questions: "Who am I?", "Am I guilty of my abandon?", "Where are my biological parents?" or "Who do I look like?" So many questions that are added to the natural period of questioning that all teenagers go through. The intense need of belonging and all the uncertainties inherent to this position can trigger off an explosive reaction which can be violent and badly interpreted by well-intentioned parents. Indeed, the teenagers can be very cruel and parents feel the injustice of the situation because they have put in so much love in the relationship. Parents have to be reassured because it is not their fault, their children are in front of a huge mountain they have to climb. All the love in this world cannot prevent such an outburst of insecurities and emotion. Here more than ever, parents have to hold on strong and prove again and again that they are present and supportive, because unconsciously their children are testing them to see if they too will abandon them one day.

Parents must not fall in the trap of feeling a lack of appreciation. Inappropriate behaviour occurs in adopted teenagers because of extreme insecurity, a feeling of being different, a sentiment of abandonment, a search for meaning, belonging and validity of their life.

Other reasons why adopted teens struggle can be linked to some high-risk pregnancies. Some adopted children's biological mother may have had an alcohol addiction problem, poor prenatal nutrition or may have lacked adequate medical care. These problems may not be known to the adoptive family, overlooked or even forgotten once the child is at home. Some of these children will have ADHD, or some other kind of emotional or psychological disorder, or show extreme impulsivity and emotional detachment. All these consequences don't show up right away, but become obvious over time and may come to a head during the teenage years.

BLENDED FAMILIES

The subtitle of this section could have been: *a time bomb or how to add fuel to fire.* Blended families are more and more frequent and the role of each member of the newly composed "tribe" has to be redefined from scratch. Family dynamics can be explosive even when the parents are married and have children together. When there is a change in that order and two families mingle, every single member has to analyse his or her new position and act appropriately.

If teenagers have extreme difficulty relating with their biological parents, trying to get loose from their authority or influence, the situation is obviously worse when dealing with a mother or father-in-law, or the mother or father's partner also called bonus parents. To make things worse, adolescents often have to deal with a total reshuffling of the family with added younger or older siblings, some of whom are going through adolescence too.

The rule of thumb is that a father-in-law or mother-in-law or bonus parent must in no case play the role of the biological father or mother when dealing with teenagers. The relationship is different by essence and must also be different in its management. They are not mothers or fathers, they are not friends either, in fact their situation is extremely complex to define. The best way to go for them is to support their partner, but not interfere frontline with teenagers that are not their own.

At a time of extreme personal tension when teenagers go against their own biological parents how could one ever imagine that they would blindly accept the interference of a man or a woman who has joined the family later in life and who didn't even know them when they were younger? To think otherwise would be ludicrous in my opinion.

In some cases, two families unite with teenagers on both sides and it would be miraculous for all of the children to have good relationships with each other instantly. It is not realistic to expect teenagers to just blend into a new family composition and live happily ever after. First of all, teens don't like the idea of their parents separating or divorcing so it is not easy to accept a new parent either. Teens often feel depression because of the change in the family, they can also feel unimportant and put aside. All this can show in expressions of anger or withdrawal. Many think that their parent has directed their love and attention towards another than themselves and feel jealous of the newcomer in the family. They are also extremely sensitive to the way their biological parent treats the bonus parent's children and can rightfully feel a lot of jealousy.

Figures show that things do go more smoothly if the re-composition of the family happens when children are young or when they are much older, having passed adolescence.

It is important for the parents to convince their teenagers that the life move they made was the right one for everyone concerned and also to show them that they can still count on all their loving attention. This will make them feel valued and will secure them in the conviction that their privileged status has not changed at all. Adolescents living in blended families need time to adjust and have the right to feel uncomfortable, sad or distressed. With enough time, counselling, support and love, they will feel more and more at ease with the new family that has built around them.

To be accepted by teenagers, the bonus parent could try to find activities or interests in common. This relationship cannot be associated to friendship but more to a certain complicity. Acknowledging similar interests and making an effort to enjoy things together may help to bond over time. Most importantly, teenagers of blended families must know that they can go to any one of the two parents, bonus or biological, if they need help.

TEENAGERS AND LOVE

Many parents don't know how to react when dealing with teenagers in love for the first time. Once again, parental reactions can go terribly wrong. An Afghan saying sets the picture: 'The magic of first love is to think it will last for ever.' It is indeed a crucial moment that parents must not underestimate. First of all, talking about teenage love means talking about profound emotions, it is also about the way the teenager sees and deals with his or her own mutating body and that of the loved one. Teenage love is primarily about the restructuring of oneself through the other.

According to Erik Erikson, 'Love for the teenager is an attempt to define one's own identity by projecting on the other diffuse images of oneself and seeing them reflecting back, and little by little getting clearer.' This is why, surprisingly, conversation and dialogue plays a key role in teenage love. It is all part of a quest for better understanding who they are.

Unfortunately, the bond that unites teenagers is often scorned at or minimised by parents or adults. Let's say that they don't take this relationship as seriously as they should.

Whether teenage love is brief in time, lasts a few years or a lifetime, it should be taken at its face value and that is an integral part of the construction of a young adult. Teenagers experience first love as a repositioning of their self as well as feelings directed towards the other. It is a way for them to learn a lot about themselves. Giving little importance to the relationship is close to denying the youth's evolution.

First love has the effect of an earthquake in so far as it affects the youth to the core, defining who he or she is and consequently validating his or her existence. As French psychologist Annie Birraux writes in *Le Corps Absolu,* a teenager in love can only envisage his body related to another's. This can develop into relationships that seem narcissistic according to the choice of the partner. For example, a girl can become very close to another one because she represents ultimately what she wants to look like or be like. It is what is called teenage transitory homosexuality. The teenager is then attracted to some other that he or she wants to resemble. Chronologically, it is firstly an attachment and only after the realisation of what is meant by this attachment.

As if all the changes in the brain and body were not enough trouble, sexuality barges in the teenager's life causing havoc. Once again the teen has to adapt. The teenager will find it difficult to regulate emotions and has to learn how to tame them.

As all of the experiences one has to go through in life, a breakup is a landmark that has a lasting impact. It is also a mandatory stage that will help the individual to mature. According to Xavier Pommereau, specialist in teenager's problems, and head of the Psychological Medical Unit in Bordeaux, 'It is an initiatory rite that all teenagers go through when they feel ready to confront their physical and psychological intimacy with the loved one.'

The adult must acknowledge the importance of a teenager suffering his or her first breakup, because the pain that he or she feels can lie dormant for years to come. Too often, parents say 'Don't worry, there are plenty of girls and boys out there, you will meet others.' By saying this, they are denying the importance of this first relationship.

If some people manage to find a satisfying relationship after a first breakup, others never get over a relationship that was aborted and wonder for years about the possible outcome that relationship would have had. It is therefore safe to say that any kind of teenage attachment has to be recognised as being meaningful, even if the pain can seem exaggerated from an adult's point of view.

Heart-broken teenagers are totally absorbed in their pain, experiencing it with passion and violence just as they do for all the other challenges that come their way.

In 2002, Catherine Mathelin, wrote an interesting essay with the collaboration of B. Costa called *Comment Survivre en Famille* ("How to Survive in a Family".) In her view, breaking up is very serious for a teenager because of the impression of having lost everything and of not being able to get over it. She advocates that adults have to be understanding because this separation revives a previous unconscious one which is the separation with the mother. She continues: 'We must all give up on total love with our mother, and on being totally accepted and taken care of.' The pain of a first breakup can be proportionate to the attachment teens still feel for their parents. Unconsciously, they are looking for an emotional substitute for the one provided by their genitors.

So when teenagers break up, the feeling of distress can be very strong. And unfortunately, this happens when they have to juggle with so many other issues such as school, family relationships, bodily transformations and so on. The impact of the breakup is then tenfold. To make things worse, they very often take on themselves all the responsibility of the failed relationship. Therefore, they will depend very much on their peers to restore their self-esteem and be ready to fall in love again.

On the other hand, if the sadness caused by a first separation turns into deep depression, this is a sign that there was already some prior profound ache and the feeling of sadness generated by the separation in only indicative of this repressed pain.

On the positive side, to experience a heart break implies that one has been able to fall in love, therefore liberating oneself from Oedipus, and has been able to love elsewhere than in the family circle, leaving childhood to become an adult. Little by little the various experiences of falling in love will show the teenager that he or she is capable of strong feelings that have to be analysed, understood and owned.

TEENAGERS AND SLEEP

Adolescence is perturbing enough for teenagers in the daytime, unfortunately it also has an impact on them at night. Parents have to review their prejudice about youngsters who are considered as being lazy because they sleep up to midday or being badly organised because they go to bed extremely late. Again, science is going to help us understand what is really going on with teenagers' particular circadian rhythm.

The latest scientific studies have made amazing discoveries. It so happens that between six and twelve years of age, sleep is of very good quality because it is composed of a lot of slow-wave sleep, i.e. deep sleep, the situation being completely different for those between thirteen and sixteen. Three elements are going to create havoc in teenagers' sleep: deterioration in the the quality of sleep, a chronic shortage of rest and a progressive deregulation.

One often hears the following advice: 'You must never wake up a sleeping baby,' but unfortunately you are never told: 'You must never wake up a sleeping teenager.' Well that is a shame because several tests have shown that after a night's sleep of the same length of time, preadolescents very rarely fall off to sleep during the following day, whereas teenagers are much more somnolent. Paradoxically, teenagers also experience difficulties in falling asleep due to their chronic sleep shortage. This is because they experience a kind of jet lag, their melatonin levels being different at adolescence. When teens should go to sleep around 11 pm, their biological clock tells them it is only 8 pm. They don't feel the need or the will to go to sleep. So when they have to get up at 7 am, their body thinks it is only 4 am. Yet at that age they do need a lot of sleep because of the hormonal turmoil going on. The consequence is that they often catch up at the weekends or holidays, sleeping all the time. They are not being lazy, they are trying to get back part of the sleep they missed out on previously because of their general sleep deficit.

Social conditioning is also negative for teenage sleep. As they often go out with friends or stay in front of their computers, consoles or smartphones until very late, youngsters will need more sleep the following day. Any excitement or attention-related activity is going to delay their sleeping time as well. A vicious circle takes place. So there is on the one hand, a natural dysfunction due to their age and on the other hand a social one because of the kind of activity they choose to do before going to sleep.

Teenagers need their sleep in the morning, whenever it is possible. It would be useless to forbid all outings or impose an unreasonable curfew. Instead they have to be informed about scientific research about their biorhythm suggesting some basic rules which will help them monitor their own sleep. Information and remediation is the way to go, but only if these come from their own understanding of the problem.

One has to explain to youngsters that adrenaline shots caused by sport they practice in the evening will not help them go to sleep either. Partying or dancing will have a similar effect. They will have to unwind before being able to go to sleep unless they have had too much alcohol, in which case they will fall asleep fast but their sleep will be of bad quality. Finally, teenagers have to be taught that their brain needs sleep to restore itself, some say from up to eleven hours. So parents have to try to hand over to teenagers the organisation of their sleeping routine by explaining all these facts. Trying to work out the problem little by little, gaining a few minutes of sleep every day. It is also a good thing to explain how slow-wave sleep consolidates what has been cognitively taken in the night before thus helping them make good use of their sleep to perform well at school. All this points to the fact that it is totally irrational to blame teenagers for their erratic sleeping habits and make them feel guilty if one doesn't take the necessary time to make them aware of what causes this behaviour and if one doesn't help them acknowledge the scientific facts at hand to be able to improve.

An interesting experiment was carried out in 2018 in two American Colleges. Realising that students were often too tired to concentrate, they decided to delay the first course by one hour letting them start their school day later than usual. Sleeping an average of 34 minutes more per week day had incredible results: there was 13% less absenteeism, 30% less late arrivals and the academic results went up by 4.5% compared to the previous year. Similar experiments are going to take place in other colleges in America and in Europe.

TEENAGERS AND TEACHERS

Teachers have to deal with students all day long, their role is complex insofar as they have to cope with their sometimes inadequate behaviour on a daily basis. On the other hand, the teacher's role is different to that of parents in many ways, making it easier for them. The fact that there is no common familial history between the teacher and the teenagers frees both parties in a way, detaching them from any prejudice or emotional issues. Having no past in common gives free range of action to the teachers who are working on virgin ground as it were. The natural distance there is between a teacher and his students is a strength compared to the tangled relationship that so often links parents to teenagers. The teachers don't face all the challenges parents do.

Teachers essentially encounter problems of discipline and also have an easier task because their actions and decisions are usually validated by the school's rules and they should get immediate support from the dean or the headmaster. To send a student out of class because of misbehaviour is not a personal decision taken by a teacher who wants to impose his or her authority, it is an action that is a logical consequence of school regulations. The teenager who rebels against such a decision knows that the one responsible is not the teacher but the institution. There are multiple cases of clashes between teenager and teachers but the situation is not the same as a teenager rebelling against his or her parents. We are here in another dimension altogether. If there is any internal coherence in the institution, the teenager knows that any other teacher would have reacted in exactly the same way. Moreover, the same punishment would be applied to any other pupil in the class. Steve Bissonnette, a Canadian teacher who currently works at TELUQ University, Quebec, holds conferences about this on a regular basis. He often talks about bad behaviour management. He stresses the fact that institutional coherence is the backbone of well-organised schools and the guarantee of reducing problems of discipline. Unfortunately, if the teenager feels he has been wrongly punished he will probably bring home his frustration and the parents will have to deal with it.

There is also a difference between what ignites bad behaviour at home and at school. More often than not, teenagers who behave badly in the classroom do so to attract attention, they need to stand out from the crowd. They are not on a journey towards freeing themselves from the authority of the teacher in the same way as they are doing at home. The school microcosm has its own specificities. Of course, some teenagers' angst does have to a certain degree an impact on school behaviour but the confrontation with the teacher is frequently caused by something radically different.

Nonetheless, some teenagers do bring their family tensions into school. I had the case of a young girl of eighteen who was unruly with all her female professors but an angel with all the men. As I was the head teacher of the class she belonged to, I had to act as a mediator between her and four teachers that she was giving hell to, and they all happened to be women. After careful dialogue with the teenager I found out that she was going through a crisis with her domineering mother and we all more or less reminded her of matriarchal authority. I suggested that we gave her some breathing space just for a few days as we would if she were our daughter. We would not ask as much from her as we would from other students, we would accept implied criticism and make out her behaviour didn't affect us that much. I suggested also that we valorised her and gave her responsibilities. After about a month, the young girl found no reason to go on pestering us, as we were not reminding her of her mother anymore. Although teachers do have a different position and role, sometimes what happens in the teenager's household does backfire on them and vice versa.

So where do we have to set the limit? Should a teacher be just a teacher or an educator? Or both? Where does the teacher's role stop and the parents' begin? Do we have to interfere when the student shows a rudeness and a lack of respect? More importantly for this analysis, what kind of emotional implication would be considered as a professional duty or as a professional mistake? The role of teachers is controversial. Some pedagogues and psychologists are of the opinion that teachers must only transmit academic knowledge, others advocate that teaching detached from any kind of emotional implication is not sufficient to build a relationship of trust which would favour teenagers' development, especially for those who find it difficult to succeed or who are showing signs of becoming school drop-outs. Alexander Sutherland Neill, the Scottish libertarian psychologist who founded Summerhill School in 1921, is known for his radical child-centred theory of education. His school looked after children who arrived as delinquents from other institutions, but with his method of education, they seemed to blossom, having found care, love, affirmation and freedom. He had strong anti-authoritarian beliefs, though his classes were traditional in practice. He was mainly focused on student happiness. He claimed: 'Our re-education schools for delinquents, with their strict methods and their punishments teach only hate. The only hope for our sick world is that a new generation is given the right to grow in love and not hate.'

Neill believed in the fundamental good intention of the human being and advocated keeping children away from the brutality and cruelty of adults. His basic principle is that it is an error to impose something on children if they don't understand the meaning behind it. The teenager must engage his own responsibility and that of others. All deviant behaviour coming from a teenager must, according to him, be subject to deep and detailed analysis to understand its motivations. Neill insists on the fact that one to one sessions with delinquent teenagers are a way of untangling misunderstandings and helping them communicate.

Even though his approach resembles the one of Jean Jacques Rousseau, Neill declares in his autobiography *Summerhill: A Radical Approach to Child Rearing* (1960) that he had read the French philosopher's work at the age of fifty, long after having started his school. In fact it was because many of his friends pointed out the similarities to him that he started to read Rousseau.

Janusz Korczak, a Polish paediatrician, founder of an orphanage and precursor of the children's rights summarises it all with this sentence, 'Delinquent teenagers need love.' His work entitled *Prawo dziecka do szacunku* (1929), which translates as: "The Right of Children to Respect", contains the gist of his philosophy. Korczak criticises vehemently the lack of consideration that the children suffer from at home and in school. He puts his finger on adults' egoism, ignorance and pride. He claims, in the name of children, their right for being what they are, that is a human being not a human being in the making, he says that they deserve respect, attention and trust. He adds: 'Can one make out that he is living? Age hierarchy does not exist.'

Published for the first time more than half a century before the ratification of the International Convention of Children's Rights (1990), this manifesto is always strikingly up to date. The following is a quotation that is used as a motto by the Korczak Association in honour of that convention. It is taken from the prologue of his work: *When I am little again* (1925).

> *You say*
> *– It is tiring to look after children*
> *You are right.*
> *You add*
> *– Because we have to put ourselves at their level. We have to bend over, stoop, make ourselves smaller.*

Here you are wrong.
It is not that which is most tiring, it is the fact to be
obliged to elevate ourselves to the level of their feelings.
To go higher, to stretch, to go on our toes, to reach higher.
In order not to harm them.

Carl Rogers was an American psychologist known for his influential psychotherapy method known as *client-centred therapy*. He was one of the founding figures of humanistic psychology. In his work *Freedom to Learn* (1972) Rogers expresses exactly what I pointed out earlier on about the right attitude to have when dealing with teenagers' provocation. Rogers invites us to 'accept the feelings of the student, even if they are disturbing (…) and to worry about the youth itself.' Concepts such as solicitude and empathic understanding are necessary. The contemporary defenders of *Care* in education follow the ideas expressed in Noddings' and Rogers' work.

All of them realise that their objective is not only a project of education but also of education itself. Following the same principles, Pierre Périer, professor of Science of Education came to identical conclusions in his writings. He led a study in 2008 in a professional secondary school in France. After having worked with students who were 'disoriented, looking for reassurance, security or complicity,' he has been able to show that preoccupations linked to authority and discipline are less important than relationships and the bonds between teachers and students. Any kind of reflexion on school violence or disruption is always linked to the engagement or disengagement of teachers towards students. He concludes by saying that the emotional dimension is an essential element in educational relationships. All the educators who were questioned in Périer's survey admitted that the human exchange is central for professionals looking after marginalised students who have entered a process of school rejection and who express themselves by absenteeism, exclusion or extreme passivity. In the same line of thought, Maël Virat, researcher in Educational Sciences, wrote a fascinating thesis in 2014, at the University of Montpellier, the subject being: "Affective dimension of the relationship teacher/student: effects on the psychosocial adaptation of teenagers (motivations, empathy, school adaptation and violence) and determining role of teachers' compassionate feeling." After deep research showing the pros and cons of the affective investment of teachers for students, he concludes: 'The affective dimension in the jobs related to education has appeared as being not only beneficial but also necessary and appropriate.' Furthermore, at the end of his thesis, Virat reports how the students portray what is for them the "best teacher". They all agree that it is the one who is ready to listen, to encourage, to show kindness and personal interest and who makes himself or herself available. On the contrary, a teacher who is too centred on the subject he or she teaches and less on the relationship with the students was considered less trustworthy.

Czech 17th-century philosopher and pedagogue Comelius had already mentioned something very similar:

> He who gives orders, teaches, counsels, reprimands must clearly show that he does so in a paternal manner. The aim of the teacher is to enhance hearts not to abase the person. If the affection is not felt by the students, they will despise the subject that is being taught with determined obstinacy.

TEENAGERS AND TRAINERS

Teachers have an easier role than parents because they can, on the one hand, take some kind of distance to solve conflicts due to their status which is external to the family and, on the other hand, because of the support of institutional rules and regulations. Professional trainers have an even more comfortable position.

Professional trainers or coaches have a legal framework that validate their actions, but they also represent an adult figure who is more appealing for teenagers. What I mean is that relationships between difficult teenagers and their professional superior, more often than not, go quite smoothly. By analysing why, we can consolidate all the things that have been said previously. The workplace is where the teenagers are going to find a new social environment, they will build their new personality around their new professional responsibilities and interests. The trainer represents an adult who is going to transmit knowledge and know-how and will be a kind of role model. In Switzerland, apprentices follow a very well-organised training which combines professional activity with school hours. Most often, the partnership between the teenage apprentice and the manager goes well. In some cases though, there are tensions and issues which cause the breaking of the contract. It is interesting to analyse what goes wrong and if we can make any parallel between this phenomenon and with the teenage issues presented earlier on in my analysis. Two Swiss authors, Jonas Masdonati and Nadia Lamamra, have tried to understand what causes the disruption. Their study, *Arrêter une formation professionnelle* (2009) is based on information collected over a six-month period from the end of 2006 to the beginning of 2007. The main focus is put on the student, not the adult. What is going on in teenagers' mind that makes him or her break the very first professional contract ever signed?

The study shows three main reasons which would cause a teenager to put an end to his or her apprenticeship. Firstly, it can be because of an erroneous conception of the working world, that is a great difference between expectations and reality, secondly it can stem from difficulties in the relationship with superiors or bad working conditions. Finally it can be caused by exclusion or harassing at the workplace.

What is of interest for our subject is the likelihood of a clash between the teenager and the superior. What comes out of Masdonati and Lamamra's work is not surprising and coincides with everything that has been pointed out previously. Here are the conclusions that can be made from the apprentices' testimonials. Young people complain very clearly about a lack of empathy and warm-heartedness on the part of the trainer, their lack of exchange, indifference and detachment. The youths need to feel that their superiors show some kind of interest in them. Another constant reproach that comes out of the survey is the lack of respect of the apprentices' private sphere when they actually need a place that they can call their own. They state that they appreciate coaches who are available and who show some kind of engagement towards them. As mentioned before, apprentices still have one foot in childhood and appreciate the care that they receive. The days when they were secured by a family structure are not so far.

Teenagers are not only on the borderline between childhood and adulthood but also between being students and professionals. They feel honoured to be in training but they are very much aware that they are still at the very bottom of the hierarchy. Positive relationships are needed in their professional surroundings which become a place for sociability, a space in which new contacts are created. This encourages the youths to participate in what is going on around them so that they can create their own atmosphere, without the filter of their family. It is their new microcosm, that belongs to them and to them alone. Just as our young boys and girls prohibit parents entering their rooms at home, they also need a personal sphere at their work place.

The survey also reveals that young apprentices detect some flaws in their trainers which correspond to parents' flaws mentioned earlier on. In order of importance, they mention a lack of patience, a lack of tact, little if no explanation, absence of positive encouragement, little to no effort of understanding and a total lack of trust.

The final revelation of the survey is that apprentices need to feel part of a team; this helps them build their professional identity which is in the making. Here we are back to what was expressed earlier on, that is the idea of disengagement from the family and engagement elsewhere.

The study ends with the one human quality that apprentices value the most in their bosses, the ability to stay calm. In the workplace, teenagers appreciate the fact of being able to make mistakes without creating an upheaval on the part of adults. Knowing they can experiment, ask questions and try again is very comforting for them and helps them learn faster. Again, we are very close to Marcia's and Lehalle's conclusions about granting a trial and error period, a moratorium.

Therefore, in the eyes of the apprentice, the professional instructor is not an authority figure that has to be confronted; rather, he is a role model. That is why conflicts on the workplace between the two generations are quite rare on the whole.

In the best of cases the apprentice will respect the adult trainer because this person represents the one he or she admires or strives to become, consciously or not. The trainer has a privileged position out of the family as well as a professional status which is a kind of validation of authority and of a certain charisma. On the other hand, it is in the interest of the trainer to look after the trainee, because in many cases, the apprentice will become a future full-time employee. He is then sowing the seeds of future success for his company. Therefore, a natural mutual respect sets in, with admiration on the one part and trust on the other. It is the same notion of trust that I mentioned earlier as being so important between parent and teenager.

An example taken from real life supports these conclusions. In New Zealand, a large corporate firm took an initiative to help its community in an original way. Instead of participating in the creation of a museum or a cultural centre, a company decided to coach pupils from a school which was in a socially underprivileged area. The firm offered its employees the chance to help teenagers who had difficulties at school. Frequent meetings were organised between professionals and students throughout one school year . Before long, the academic results of these young students went up dramatically and so did their self-esteem.

This example shows that sometimes our society tries to solve problems but doesn't always choose the best ways to do so.

Augmenting financial aid would have surely helped the school but the human input had a much stronger impact. The teens felt someone was caring for them and were ready to take time to help them reveal their potential.

CONCLUSION

I would like to conclude with a warning. We have seen that there is no adolescent without some kind of crisis. However, there are two attitudes that are equally dangerous. The first one is to think that any strange behaviour could be pathological and that one has to interfere straight away without letting time play its role. The other is to ignore more serious signs which show that teenagers are really in need of professional help. Severe cases of depression, eating disorders like anorexia and bulimia, or hard drug addictions are issues that need to be addressed immediately. Such cases need the help and expertise of professionals to avoid serious outcomes. Only a medical framework and close guidance can help in those circumstances.

I have unfortunately witnessed a family situation in which a young boy of eighteen put an end to his life by jumping off a bridge although he had an extremely loving and caring family. It was the effect of long-term drug consumption that prevailed in the end, and all parental efforts proved useless.

On a happier note, I would like to end this part by saying that what we have to keep in mind is the richness of adolescence and the fecundity of this wonderful period. Indeed, at the intersection between childhood and adulthood, teenagers can have a double perspective, they can still look in two directions, not belonging to one anymore but not completely absorbed by the other. This moment filled with complexity is productive because of the profusion of questioning and transformations that it beholds.

One can say that adolescence is a journey through so many feelings and stages, all of which will have to be dealt with, for the individual to be able to finally step on the more stable path of adulthood.

Our youths represent the future, so let's believe in them, let's help them grow so that they are able to define themselves and thrive. Our unconditional and discreet support is the fundamental element for their self-construction and it will have, as a consequence, the continuation of the unique relationship which should naturally exist between parents and their children.

When asked about my role as a parent or a teacher, I answer that I see myself merely as a facilitator, that is someone who helps others progress, helping them to function effectively, supporting them every step of the way as they pursue their own personal objectives.

Each time that I think about my parents, it is with love and extreme gratitude. Without ever having consulted a book on pedagogy, they were always perfect in their way of dealing with my brother and myself, helping us grow with a feeling of love, security, trust, understanding and encouragement at each and every stage of our life. They behaved the exact same way with their six grandchildren. I wish that every teenager had such support and love. I also hope that this book has helped some parents find their way in feeling more confident about their role of a lifetime.

PART II

SOME ILLUSTRATIONS OF ADOLESCENTS IN ANGLO-SAXON, FRENCH AND ITALIAN LITERATURE

Most teen behaviours mentioned in this study have been represented in literature. Fiction has been inspired by the wonderful state of contradictory emotions that is characteristic of youth. Love is omnipresent, but also other feelings that are magnified during this period of life, sadness, anger, revolt, indecision, foolishness, etc. Let's journey through literature in general and explore some stereotypical portrayals of teenagers in various literary genres and periods before proceeding into a deeper analysis of some selected works.

If we consider how teenagers occupy a place in literature there are representations of young men taking their destiny in hand, fighting perilous battles like Lancelot in *Le Chevalier à la Charrette* witten by Chrétien de Troyes in the 12th century or like Rodrigue in *Le Cid* written by Corneille in the 17th century. On the other hand, the young girls are mostly described as victims in the Greek tragedies in which they are often obliged to obey the divine laws or the political constraints like Sophocles' *Antigone* or Racine's *Iphigénie*. They are also submissive and obedient to the will of their father or husband like Cordelia in *King Lear* by Shakespeare. In traditional fairy tales, they are pursued as in Charles Perrault's *Peau d'Âne*, exploited as in *Cinderella* or even threatened with death as in *Snow White*. In the 19th Century they are mistreated like Cosette in *Les Misérables* (Victor Hugo) or humiliated like Coelina in *Coelina ou l'Enfant Mystère* (Guilbert de Pixerécourt) before being saved.

However, we do have examples of young girls who take their independence as in L'abbé Prévost's *Manon Lescault* (1731) or Emile Zola's *Nana* (1880). Unfortunately they often finish living a life of prostitution in their search for independence or end up coping with early pregnancy and being rejected like the heroine in *Tess of the D'Ubervilles* (1891) by Thomas Hardy.

The 19th century is filled with young fictional characters becoming adults with the *Bildungsroman* (literally: "novel of formation, of education"). It was coined in 1819 by philologist Karl Morgenstern during his university lectures; Wilhelm Dilthey revived it 1870 and popularised it in 1905. It is roughly equivalent to the *coming-of-age novel*. *Wilhelm Meister's Apprenticeship* by Johann Wolfgang Goethe (1795) is usually cited as the first work of that kind. Flourishing in German-speaking states, the *Bildungsroman* has also had extensive influence in Europe through the translation of German works.

The very essence of a Bildungsroman is the relating of a young character who is going to travel both geographically or mentally in search of answers to life's questions. The aim is to find oneself, to try to solve the equation between auto-determination and constraints that come from the outside world or society. Usually at the beginning of the narration there is an emotional loss which projects the protagonist on his journey. The final aim is maturity. The protagonist is going to go through many mental struggles and will have to adjust his inner aspirations to some basic societal constraints. This process is contrary to the ideas presented by more optimistic authors such as Robert Musil who writes in his unfinished book *The Man Without Qualities* (1930–1943): 'A man is never happier than when he manages to behave in the way that he had imagined as a teenager.'

It is worth mentioning Arthur Rimbaud for the 19th century, although he is not a fictional character, because as a poet he embodies all the revolt that is typical of adolescence. He himself was an adolescent when he wrote his poetry and he set a kind of trend that adolescence is a revolution that cannot be overlooked. What is fascinating is that instead of seeing adolescence as a passage towards the more stable period of adulthood, he valorised it as being the best period itself because of its profusion and folly. He showed that adulthood is full of falsehood and lies and adolescence is the only time which is really worthwhile; it is the moment when one can give free rein to imagination and poetic creation. In his poems he criticised his parents, an authoritative mother and an absent father; he also puts the blame on all the structures meant to canalise youth, such as religious ceremonies or military obligations which kill young soldiers, like in the poem "Le Dormeur du Val" (1870). For him anything that is institutional is bad, even marriage that kills love. It is as though adolescence is better than childhood which is too naïve and adulthood which is too corrupt. It is a period both wonderful and frightening. Rimbaud himself experienced all the excesses of adolescence with an uncontrolled use of alcohol, drugs and also dissolute living and verbal violence expressed in his poems.

At the beginning of the 20th century there was a new social group composed of adolescents which seemed to be distinct from that of adults. This new category of people tended to be reluctant in obeying social rules or adults' requirements. Margaret Mitchell's Scarlet O'Hara in *Gone with the Wind* (1936), who rules her microcosm in a very controlling way, is the epitome of a young woman knowing what she wants and how to get it during the American Civil War. Much later, in *Le Bal des Voleurs* written by Jean Anouilh in 1938, Juliet takes the reins of a situation to turn it to her advantage. Some young girls not only confront their parents but take revenge on them like Antoinette Kampf – *Kampf* meaning "battle" in German – in *Le Bal* written by Irène Némirovsky in 1929.

What comes through is the universality of statements made either implicitly or explicitly about teenagers throughout various literary representations. I purposely avoided following any chronological road map in my study to feel free to let myself be driven here and there, according to examples that came to my mind spontaneously. I also found that connections could be made between some teenage portraits although they belonged to very different literary periods or genres.

We have seen in the first part of the book that adult authority is put into question by adolescents and that any advice coming from them is, more often than not, rejected or made fun of. The ironic quote of Mark Twain makes me laugh each time I read it: 'When I was a boy of 14 my father was so ignorant I could hardly stand to have the old man around. But when I got to be 21, I was astonished at how much the old man learnt in 7 years.'

Shakespeare was a master in portraying the complexity inherent in adolescence. We can read in *A Winter's Tale:* 'I would there were no age between sixteen and three-and-twenty, or that youth would sleep out the rest; for there is nothing in the between but getting wenches with child, wronging the ancientry, stealing, fighting.' And a little later: 'Would any but these boiled brains of nineteen and two-and-twenty hunt in this weather?'

He managed to describe the terrifying beauty of adolescence with such analytical finesse that his portraits are ageless. For example, the most recent up-to-date descriptions of teenagers can be put side to side with the portrayals of Romeo and Juliet. In the play the author shows both the magnificence and strength of teenagers along with their bold, erratic behaviour, so typical of their age and which can cause incredible annoyance to adults.

Shakespeare reveals their wonders but also their contradictions, absurdities and terrible flaws. The main characteristic being that their rebellion is a losing battle because it goes against world order (which could be assimilated to mature thinking in some cases). There are two possible outcomes, either the youth dies in a moment of glory in the tragedies like *Romeo and Juliet* or *Hamlet* or he matures and changes as in the comedies like *A Midsummer Night's Dream* or *All's Well that Ends Well*.

His portrait of Juliet is a wonderful representation of a young girl who shifts from childhood to adolescence. She is almost fourteen years of age at the beginning of the play and is totally submissive to the wishes and desires of her parents. Little by little she gains assurance to reject them and take her own decisions, even if these are extreme. Her interactions with Romeo are representative of her rebellion. She will break three things that linked her to her former identity: her nurse, her parents and her social position in Verona. She moves rapidly towards a state of independence and revolt, questioning her parents' values. She will teach herself self-confidence and will get to an impressive final stage of decision making. In Act I, scene 3, she already shows signs of independence towards her nurse and in her exchanges with Romeo, a strength of character and a direction that she is going to follow whatever comes her way. The judgment Juliet makes of adults in Act II scene 5 is unequivocal:

> If she was young and passionate, she'd move as fast as a ball. My words would bounce her to my sweet love and his words would bounce her back to me. But a lot of old people act like they're already dead-sluggish, slow, fat and colourless, like lead.

As for Romeo, he is a beautiful example of impulsivity, extreme in thoughts and actions. Shakespeare makes him mature at a slower pace than Juliet, although the whole action takes place within five days only. Romeo is presented to us as a narcissistic teen, egotist and impulsive. He starts out as a rejected lover, distressed because Rosalind does not love him. His initial words set in sonnets are pompous and show his inexperience. When he sees Juliet, he starts his transition to a more mature youth, although he still has a long way to go. His lines change too, he shifts into verse. Unfortunately, his maturing will never overcome his destructive impulsiveness, which will cause his death.

Hamlet is the other portrayal of teenager's sensitivity. This play is extremely interesting because although one focuses on the hero Hamlet, there is another teenager in the play whose development is much more interesting for our analysis. The fact is that Hamlet is around 33 years of age in the play, Shakespeare doesn't give us the information directly but we can deduce it. Although Hamlet is at an age when he should act as an adult, he has a typical teenager's behaviour. The most blatant example of this is when he thinks in extremes: 'To be or not to be.' He seems obsessed with his mother's sexual relations with Claudius.

Somehow his mother's remarriage upsets him more than his father's death. Hamlet is incapable of half-measure, his world is either black or white. His obsession with his mother's physical relationship with his uncle is seen by many as an Oedipal complex. It is quite obvious that Hamlet is jealous of the attention his mother is giving Claudius. But what is even more fascinating in this play, is the portrait of the icon of a spoilt adolescence represented by Ophelia. She has no control over her short life and will not have any over her death either, she is constantly pushed about between her father, her brother, her king and her lover. She is never given a chance of being listened to or even considered as a person. She finally gives in under all the pressure. Just like Romeo and Juliet were victims of the ancestral hate of their two families, Ophelia is a victim of the adult world surrounding her. She has no autonomy, no power of decision. Unlike Juliet who matures and makes her own decisions, Ophelia is literally drowned in a world of submission and neglect.

King Lear is another play which is worth mentioning. Here it is the father's authority and blindness which cause tragedy. Scene after scene, Lear goes on misinterpreting his children's statements and makes terrible mistakes. He will see far too late that his only truthful and sincere daughter is Cordelia. Interestingly, there is a total reversal of roles at the end of the play when Cordelia starts taking on the position of the parent, or more specifically the mother looking after and consoling her father who, having lived so long, has become a child again, at the mercy of others and of his alienated mind.

Blindness is not just the flaw of irresponsible fathers. Some women are totally incapable of acknowledging the fact that their sons are growing up and need to become adults. This is the very subject of the powerful autobiographical novel *Sons and Lovers* (1913) by D. H. Lawrence. Here, not only do we have exposed the Oedipal complex, as has often been pointed out, but we have two young men whose teenage years are destroyed by their mother. The successive affective issues that Mrs Morel has to endure have a direct incidence on the development of her two sons William and Paul, who do not have the freedom to become adults and to love elsewhere than in the domestic realm. Disappointed by the intellectual shortcomings of her husband and by his lack of demonstrative affection, she lays all her affection on her sons at the very moment in their lives when they need to take some distance.

In a normal relationship between a mother and a son, at the very critical stage, the personal identity of the youth should already be solid enough in its construction so that he can redirect his attention from his mother and focus it on another female identity. He will then become an adult and will start a natural relationship with another woman. Between William and his mother, this is impossible because of the exclusive relationship that the mother has woven. This is what Mrs Morel says about her son's girlfriend: 'I can't bear it, I could let another woman – but not her – she'd leave me no room, not a bit of room.' It is clear that no other girl would ever fit in her categorisation, as the only acceptable object of her son's affection is herself.

What best contrast than this wonderful letter written by Steinbeck to his son Thom who wanted to share with his father his strong attachment for a young girl named Susan. Even if it sounds as though this love is a teenage love despite what Steinbeck writes, the father's tact is admirable in so far as it respects the importance and the urgency of this affectionate attachment. This letter is making the statement that even teenage love is legitimate and should be treated as such. It is one of the most beautiful pieces of unsolicited parental advice on love ever given.

New York
November 10, 1958

Dear Thom:

We had your letter this morning. I will answer it from my point of view and of course Elaine will from hers.

First – if you are in love – that's a good thing – that's about the best thing that can happen to anyone. Don't let anyone make it small or light to you.

Second – There are several kinds of love. One is a selfish, mean, grasping, egotistical thing which uses love for self-importance. This is the ugly and crippling kind. The other is an outpouring of everything good in you – of kindness and consideration and respect – not only the social respect of manners but the greater respect which is recognition of another person as unique and valuable. The first kind can make you sick and small and weak but the second can release in you strength, and courage and goodness and even wisdom you didn't know you had.

You say this is not puppy love. If you feel so deeply – of course it isn't puppy love.

But I don't think you were asking me what you feel. You know better than anyone. What you wanted me to help you with is what to do about it – and that I can tell you.

Glory in it for one thing and be very glad and grateful for it.

The object of love is the best and most beautiful. Try to live up to it.

If you love someone – there is no possible harm in saying so – only you must remember that some people are very shy and sometimes the saying must take that shyness into consideration.

Girls have a way of knowing or feeling what you feel, but they usually like to hear it also.

It sometimes happens that what you feel is not returned for one reason or another – but that does not make your feeling less valuable and good.

Lastly, I know your feeling because I have it and I'm glad you have it.

We will be glad to meet Susan. She will be very welcome. But Elaine will make all such arrangements because that is her province and she will be very glad to. She knows about love too and maybe she can give you more help than I can.

And don't worry about losing. If it is right, it happens – The main thing is not to hurry.

Nothing good gets away.

Love,
Fa

John Steinbeck. Edited by Elaine Steinbeck and Robert Wallsten. *Steinbeck: A Life in Letters.* (1975).

Another letter from Alexandre Dumas to his son also enchanted me when I read it. Although there are some intrinsic contradictions. On the one hand, the father says everything to valorise his son, treating him like an adult, on the other hand he is giving him a list of directives that would have made any teenager giddy, even at that period! I find the tone respectful and I love the way the father promises that they will find a proper professional direction together for the son even if the direction the son is going to take leaves very little doubt.

My dear child

You letter pleased me a great deal, like all the letters in which I see that you are doing well. The Latin verse that you are given to do and of which you ask my opinion, are not very important. Nonetheless, learn their rhythm so that you can scan the language and feel the harmony of the language of Virgil and the lack of harmony of those of Harotius. Once you get the hang of the rhythm of the language it will be useful to you if ever you have to speak it – in Hungary for example where any peasant can speak Latin. Learn Greek well to be able to read Homer, Sophocles, Euripide in the original text and to be able to learn modern Greek in three months – finally practice German pronunciation: later on you will learn English and Italian. Then, after you will have learnt all that, we shall judge ourselves, and together, the career that you are suited for.

By the way don't neglect the art of drawing. Tell Charlieu to give you not only Shakespeare, but also Dante and Schiller to read.

Don't worry about the verse that you are taught in college. Those kinds of teacher's verses are not worth a thing. Study the Bible not only as a religious but historical and poetic book – Sacy's translation is the best. Find in the bible, through it's translation, the wonderful poetry that it contains – in Saül, in Joseph. Read Corneille, learn some of it by heart. Corneille is not always poetic but his language is always beautiful, colourful and concise. Tell Colin to have Hachette give you four volumes entitled Rome during Augustus' century. Read Hugo and Lamartine, but only the « Meditations » and the « Harmonies » and make your own selection of things that you find beautiful or bad, you will show them to me on my return. Finally work well and find good rest in the very variety of your work. Look after your health and be good.

Farewell my dear child. I am telling Dommange to give you twenty francs for Christmas.

Kisses
Alex. D.

P-S

Go to see Tresse, get the following on my account: Hugo's poetry and his plays, and the Molière of Panthéon.

I will give you Lamartine when I come back.

Read a lot of Molière. He is a great model of the language of Louis XIV. Learn by heart some passages of Tartuffe, of the Femmes Savantes and of The Misanthrope. Other things have been done differently and will still be done differently but nothing will have a better style than that. Learn by heart Charles the Fifth's monologue in Hernani.

And the discourse of St-Vallier from Le Roi s'amuse; the monologue of the 5th Act of Triboulet, the speech of Angelo on Venice, the speech of Nangis to Louis the 13th in Marion Delorme – finally from me, you can also learn the story of Stella's in Caligula and the lion hunt of Yacoub, as well as all the scene of the 3rd Act between the count, Charles the 7th and Agnès Sorel. Those are the ancient and modern writers that I suggest you study first, then later on, you will go from detail to the whole.

Farewell, you see that I treat you as a big boy and that I speak to you with reason. You are going to be 16 years old and it is normal that I address you this way.

Your health means more than anything, it is in the future source of everything.

Alexandre Dumas, *Lettres à mon fils. Le Temps Retrouvé.* (1839)

The conflict between mother and son as depicted in *Sons and Lovers* between Mrs Morel and William and Paul is treated in a very different way in Alberto Moravia's novel *Agostino* written in 1944 and *La Disubbidienzia* in 1948. We have the same problem but portrayed the other way around.

Agostino is the story of a sensitive, cloistered boy who, beyond all sense of proportion, loves and idolises his youthful widowed mother. The shock of finding he is not the centre of his mother's universe is more than Agostino can stand. In an instinctive fumbling effort to gain self-respect and values, Agostino joins a gang of older boys who callously supply him with a quick and drastic sexual education.

Agostino finds he has won knowledge without wisdom and in the words of Moravia, 'He has lost his first estate without having succeeded in winning another.'

This short novel is considered to be among Moravia's most successful works. While Agostino is becoming aware of his own sexuality, he watches his mother drift towards an affair with a young man named Renzo, and is himself suspected by the boys of having succumbed to the homosexual life-guard Saro, and is turned away from the local house of prostitution because of his childish appearance.

He is trying to figure out his relationship with his mother but is having great difficulty in doing so and ultimately in understanding what is going on in his mind. Agostino is wondering:

> But why did he so desire not to love his mother anymore? Why did he hate his love for her? Maybe he was pushed by a feeling of having been deceived, to have thought she was different to what she was in reality; maybe it would be easier not to love her anymore rather than not being able to love her without suffering.

In *La Disubbidienza*, Moravia depicts Luca, who is more sophisticated, knowing and introspective than Agostino. When his active mind questions the conventions and routine of everyday life he gradually comes to the conclusion that life is a monstrous conspiracy – a plot to make one conform at the expense of one's soul. His answer will be a complete negation of the reason for living – an austere and adolescent reaction that leads him to the brink of death itself: 'This temptation for committing suicide didn't frighten him, it didn't seem absurd either; according to him,

it was the normal outcome of a terrible feeling of helpless-
ness which was upsetting him.'

He is then saved physically and mentally by a violent illness
and an unexpected romance after which he finally reaches
some degree of maturity.

Alberto Moravia's wife from 1941 to 1962, Elsa Morante,
also wrote a novel in 1957 which was very much concerned
with teenage turmoil: *The Island of Arturo. Memoirs of an
Adolescent.* She portrays the life of a teenager, who lost his
mother when she gave birth to him. Arturo is lonely and
untamed. He will go through an initiation that will lead
him to solving the mysteries of life itself. The quality of the
novel is its capacity to describe the development of the child
through all the steps of adolescence. First, there is repulsion
against the other sex, then the discovery of love but also
deception in love relationships and in his father figure. The
island, surrounded by the sea represents all the world of his
childhood. The passage to adolescence with the discovery of
truths and disillusions causes in him a deep disenchantment
until, he too, will become an adult. When he decides to leave
the island, he metaphorically bids farewell to his childhood
fantasies. Arturo says: 'Now that time has passed, I try to
understand the feelings which began growing strangely in
my heart… but still today, I realise that I am incapable of
distinguishing the forms that were so mixed inside of me…'

Unravelling mixed feelings is partly the subject of *A Portrait
of the Artist as a Young Man*, in which we have the interesting
point of view of the development of individual conscious-
ness. The author, James Joyce, transcribes the thoughts
and sensations that go through a character's mind rather
than simply describing those sensations from the external

standpoint of an observer. We actually see the development of Stephen's mind as he juggles with sensations, emotions and experiences.

What is interesting regarding our analysis of teenagers is that we see the difference between the way the mind works when one is a child, a teenager or an adult. The very young Stephen is only capable of describing his world in simple words and phrases. He shows the typical lack of attention to cause and effect characteristic of a child's view. Later when Stephen is a teenager, obsessed with religion, he is able to think in a clearer, more adult manner. It is when Stephen is at university that he seems really truly rational. By the end of the novel, Joyce renders a portrait of a mind that has achieved emotional, intellectual and artistic maturity.

> I will tell you what I will do and what I will not do. I will not serve that in which I no longer believe, whether it calls itself my home, my fatherland, or my church: and will try to express myself in some mode of life or art as freely as I can and as wholly as I can, using for my defence the only arms I allow myself to use: silence, exile and cunning.

Not going along with something one does not longer believe in is part of the problem in the short story entitled "Teenage Wasteland" written by American writer Anne Tyler in 1983. The title comes from a song entitled "Baba O'Riley" by The Who. The song was released in 1971 and also contains the theme of adolescent growth. It is about relationships between parents and teenagers and how their worlds do not seem to intersect due to difficulties in understanding one another. Their relationship gradually disintegrates.

Daisy Cobie is a housewife who once was a teacher, her fifteen-year old son Donny isn't doing well at school, showing no motivation or interest. His father figure is not very present in his life. As the story unfolds, Daisy is summoned to Donny's school to discuss his academic difficulties. At first Daisy feels responsible but quickly realises that Donny might need a tutor to help him. Cal Beadle starts coaching the adolescent who enjoys his sessions with this personalised help. It is the first time there is a real connection between the teenager and an adult. Donny makes progress constructing his identity but his school results are still bad. The mother then decides to put him in a public school, where the marks get better but Donny's personal situation and equilibrium are obviously worsening. Finally, the teenager disappears and is never heard of again.

It is important to note that none of Donny's actions are actually witnessed by the audience. They are only spoken about. This indirect characterisation puts us, as it were, in the position of the teenager's mother, wondering what is happening to him. The image with which Tyler closes the story is subtle and moving. Lying awake at night, Daisy tries to understand what has happened and has a vision of Cal's yard, where a neighbour's fence casts narrow shadow bars across the spring grass. As she drifts off to sleep, she recalls that scene, the stripes of sunlight's 'as white as bones, bleached and parched and cleanly picked.' It is a fearful image, one that Tyler does not explain, leaving it to the reader to interpret as an expression of Daisy's defeat and despair in trying to bridge the gap with her son.

Back to the 19th century, In Jane Austen's novels, we see parents who are portrayed in a very different manner. They have great difficulty in disciplining their teenage daughters, not only because of the financial and social projections that they try to impose on them, but also because of the unpredictable and rebellious behaviour of their young girls. Faced with the clear determination of parents who never cease to try to organise weddings which would bring not only money but social status to their daughters, we have an explosion of hormonal reactions on the part of the heroines who adopt all the typical postures of erratic female teen-agers. Impulsive decisions, mistakes of interpretation and prejudice, understatements and vexations are all part of the joyful but stressful atmosphere of these families in which the girls often get what they want putting to the test the nervous balance of parents, of whom, Mrs Bennet in *Pride and Prejudice* (1815) is probably the best incarnation.

In it we have Elizabeth, a young girl of twenty-years old who does exactly what she wants and who has a quick answer to everything. She tears apart all good behaviour codes and places love as the main ingredient in the recipe of marriage, instead of social position or financial security, which were the norm at that period. Even if her views on marriage are rightful, she makes numerous misjudgements which she will realise later on in the story. Her younger sisters, Kitty, seventeen and Lydia, fifteen are also the very incarnations of youth's immaturity and egotism.

In *Emma* (1815), Jane Austen presents another protagonist who, just like Elizabeth in *Pride and Prejudice* and Anne in *Persuasion* (1817), is unconventional and autonomous, marrying the man she loves, breaking the codes of the 19th century.

Jane Austen is thirty-five years of age when she writes her main works, the first of which is *Sense and Sensibility* (1811).

She appears as a reasonable authoress, pious and solitary, writing under the pseudonym of "A Lady". However, many people ignore that her first literary productions which were written when she was only fifteen, already describe admirably teenage irrational behaviour. Her early works are little masterpieces which portray characters who have particular disdain and opposition to any kind of authority. It is only in 1922, more than a century after Jane Austen's death, that the first substantial collection of her first writings will be published.

In these texts written between 1787 and 1793, the characters get up to mischief, either drinking too much, having hysterical tantrums and even committing a crime. We can also see intense friendship unravel, strange love relationships and very often an obvious scorn for the elders. These miniature novels were meant to be read in family gatherings and only in her very close social circle. One of her heroines even announces in a very controlled way to a friend that now that she has assassinated her father and mother she was about to murder her sister! We also have an alcoholic character in *Jack and Alice*. Another character brags by saying: 'It is my greatest boast that I have incurred the displeasure of my father!'

Let's remind ourselves that at that period of time, Mary Wollstonecraft, a school teacher, authoress, philosopher and feminist had very probably had an influence on Jane Austen's ideas. Indeed, we find the desire of autonomy and of unleashed discourse and plain speaking in most of her heroines throughout her writings.

In the small novel of 1792, entitled *Kitty or the Bower*, Austen, who was only sixteen, writes with incredible candour about marriage and sexuality:

> But do you call it lucky, for a girl of genius and feeling to be sent in quest of a husband to Bengal, to be married there to a man of who disposition she has no opportunity of judging till her judgement is of no use to her, who may be a tyrant, or a fool or both for what she knows to the contrary. Do you call that fortunate?

Thus, Jane Austen as a teenager wrote funny and fine stories which contrast with the psychological reality and discipline of her future novels. But in between the lines, we do find in her best known works, here and there, some remnants of erratic teenagehood. In *Sense and Sensibility*, Elinor Dashwood asks for a glass of strong alcohol to be able to cope with her sister Mariane's hysterics. She says: 'If you will give me leave, I will drink the wine myself'. Or in *Pride and Prejudice*, Elizabeth Bennet takes the irrational decision to cross over fields on a crazy whim to see her sister Jane at Netherfield Park,'crossing field and field at a quick pace, jumping over stiles and springing over puddles.'

Although they may be linked by their early 19th century British backgrounds and legions of devotees, Jane Austen and Charlotte Brontë were very different both in background and literary production. What is certain is that they both made, in their own way, an immense contribution to literature.

I read *Jane Eyre* when I was eighteen, and it was a wonderful experience. I kept the book for years at hand. Little did I understand at the time what Charlotte Brontë's novel had brought me and why I was so fascinated by it. In retrospect, I think I have pinpointed some, if not all of the aspects of its mesmerising attraction.

This gem of a gothic novel is far from being outdated and seems to have gone through a revival lately. It even appears on the list of favourites by *YA readers*! Not only is it a *beautiful classic* but it has become a *classic young adult's favourite book*. To be able to understand why female young adults turn to *Jane Eyre* today, we have to give it a closer look.

Jane Eyre published in 1847, was one of the first novels that set out to explore what if feels like to be a child. Unlike Charles Dickens' slightly earlier work, *Oliver Twist* (1838), it is recounted by the heroine herself, supposedly in adulthood, but with all the intensity of immediate experience. The novel is quite a revolution if we think of the way children were depicted in Victorian times in *Ellen, or the Naughty Girl Reclaimed*, a picture book in which a disobedient girl learns to control herself and becomes a quiet, obedient daughter, who is 'anxious her dear mamma to please.' For the Victorians, children who did not control themselves could finish up leading a life of crime and depravity, or could become complete maniacs. The same strict control was to be applied to young women whether by wearing a corset or obeying their husbands.

The Victorians were very much concerned with the question when one stopped being a child and became an adult. It was during the Victorian era that the years from age thirteen to twenty-four came to be regarded as a distinct epoch in individual development. The word "adolescence" came into vogue in the late nineteenth century, and the first major sociological study of it, G. Stanley Hall's *Adolescence*, appeared in 1905. Consequently, it was regarded as a complex social, psychological and moral process.

In her anger and passion, Jane Eyre is far removed from the conventional model of the Victorian child who should be "seen and not heard". Instead, she is part of new, emerging, more sympathetic attitude to childhood, which stressed that adults should pay attention to the feelings and sufferings of children. She is a defiant child who is fully convinced of the rightfulness of her rebellion. She uses strong words comparing her mood to that of 'a rebel slave' with her 'heart in insurrection.' Jane has no father or mother to rebel against as she is an orphan, but she has an aunt who treats her badly and who is the recipient of one of the best child's tirade in English literature in my opinion. In Chapter 4, young Jane declares prior to her departure from Gateshead for Lowood School

> I am glad you are no relation of mine. I will never call you aunt as long as I live. I will never come to visit you when I am grown up; and if any one asks me how I liked you, and how you treated me, I will say the thought of you makes me sick, and that you treated me with miserable cruelty... You think I have no feelings, and that I can do without one bit of love or kindness: but I cannot live so: and you have no pity. I shall remember how you thrust me back... into the red room... and that punishment made me suffer because your wicked boy struck me – knocked me down for nothing. I will tell anybody who asks me questions this exact tale.

Jane then gives us an insight of the effect this outburst has on her:

> When I had finished, this reply, my soul began to expand, to exult, with the strangest sense of freedom, of triumph, I ever felt. It seemed as if an invisible bond had burst and that I had struggled out into unhoped-for liberty...

But then Jane gets older and is eighteen years of age for most of the novel. *Jane Eyre* is a book about finding one's identity in the face of adversity, it is a book about coming of age, a Bildungsroman. What makes her the quintessential adolescent is that everything is new to her, she has no experience of love , social exchange or of city life, and no family security to depend on. She has everything to learn and has to do it herself, with no exterior help. Charlotte Brontë writes of a character balanced between childhood and maturity. In fact, she uses the tension of this balance again and again to give her story energy. The fact that Jane is a maturing youth taking her first steps into a wider world, makes her story particularly resonant for young adult readers. Moreover, although the novel does not contain any explicit sex, it explores female adolescent desire so openly that some implied connotations shocked its Victorian readers.

The relationship between Jane and Edward Rochester is fiery to say the least. Jane somehow manages to overpower him although he seems so much stronger, experienced and intimidating. She develops little ways of manipulating him which will make him totally addicted to her and indifferent to the more beautiful and socially compatible Blanche Ingram.

Before her passionate relationship, Jane was also very much attracted to Helen Burns, a girl just a few years older than her who was sharing the awful conditions in Lowood School. We have here the typical teenage peer relationship, with two opposite personalities which attract. Helen is a foil to Jane, as her constant understanding and forgiveness contrast with Jane's rebelliousness and revolt. Moreover, while Helen knows she will find happiness after death, Jane is determined to find it on earth. What Helen tells Jane during their conversation the night of her death is in total opposition with what Jane had heard from adults. This will influence and mould Jane's outlook on life from then on.

When reading *Jane Eyre* one has to make a parallel with Charlotte Brontë who also went through a teenage crisis, putting her feelings in writing. Obviously the Brontës did not intend their books to be published for a teenage audience specifically, this marketing category would not exist for another century, however we can't help thinking she wouldn't have disapproved. She also wants her readers to be on the side of the child against adult tyranny.

The more I think about the novel the more it seems clear that it has a lot to offer young girls today, the whole debate about being your own provider, not depending one hundred per cent on a man was very new at the time and resonates with modern female aspirations.

Let's shift from 19th century England to a single parent family in France in the pre-revolutionary context of "Mai 68". With the novel *Bonjour Tristesse* (1954) Françoise Sagan takes us into another world altogether. Not only the heroine Cécile is a teenager of seventeen but the authoress was only eighteen herself when she wrote this little master-piece of social analysis. This double perspective is fascinating because at that time, adolescence was not scrutinised and analysed like it is today. But the publication of the book forced critics to start getting their minds around the phenomenon. The instant success of the novel was due to its rebellion against the French middle class's decorum and way of life. The novel also describes folly, disrespect and risk-taking, all typical teenage postures . François Mauriac didn't approve of the book and criticised it openly, condemning 'the immoral behaviour of female adolescence.'

Bonjour Tristesse, is the story of a happy relationship between a father Raymond and his daughter Cécile which will be marred by the arrival of a character who wants to control the young girl. This will lead to dramatic consequences. Cécile appreciates the relationship she has with her father. It is excessive and marginal but coincides exactly with what she wants at that period of her life. They both get along fine, respecting each other's freedom, they also share an irresistible desire for living without any kind of restriction or prohibition.

Raymond lets his daughter do whatever she wishes in her private life. The crisis happens when Anne, a girlfriend of his, is going to show inclinations for taking on the role of Cécile's mother who passed away. By wanting to take control over Cécile's life which was carefree up to then, she is going to cause havoc.

Cécile's remark is very common to all teenagers who rebel against their parents. What she says summarises Marcia's identity theory beautifully. She asks for 'freedom to think, even if [she] think[s] wrongly, and as little as [she] please[s].' She continues: 'the freedom of choosing my life myself as well as my own identity. I cannot say the freedom to be myself because I was nothing but malleable dough, but I wanted the freedom of being able to refuse any given mold.'

Young Cécile is frightened that her father's new girlfriend Anne is going to guide her, taking away her autonomy and giving her ready made answers to all her questions. To escape this authority of her future step-mother, Cécile is going to orchestrate a terrifying scenario, which will result in Anne's death in a car accident which resembles a suicide.

In *Bonjour Tristesse,* we also find a passage which shows the typical awkwardness of teenagers faced with their changing body. Cécile compares herself unconsciously to her father's conquests, Elsa and Anne, who are both beautiful women. She has no choice but to accept her father's hurtful remarks when he compares her to a 'skinny chicken' or to 'a grasshopper who is too thin.' When Cécile thinks that she could be pregnant she says, 'In any case, I couldn't imagine myself being pregnant with the thin and hard body that I had... for once, I was happy with my teenage anatomy.'

Françoise Sagan made her mark in literature at a period when she found enormous response from the teenage audience. Young girls who were one hundred per cent receptive to the intimate and daring confidences of the heroine. The very young feminine public instantly devoured the book with passion because they found in it the expression of their own feelings that were impossible to express such as their desire for sexual freedom which is cautioned by Cécile in the novel and later by the authoress herself. Sagan became popular very quickly, having the support of the young feminine generation and the backup of Simone de Beauvoir, famous feminist and author who published *Memoirs of a Dutiful Daughter* (*Les Mémoires d'une Jeune Fille Rangée*) in 1958.

The bawdiness of Cécile echoes the lewdness of another young girl in a highly controversial novel, *Lolita*, by Vladimir Nabokov, published in 1955. Here we have all the perversion of an adult who makes the most of the vulnerability of youth to satisfy his own fantasies. For some readers, this novel is painful to read because of the abject behaviour of Humbert Humbert.

But what I find interesting in this novel is Nabokov's beautifully original syntax and choice of words but also the perfect description of teenage attachment opposed to adult's love. Indeed, as stated in my analysis, teenage love is part and parcel of teenager identity-building, but Humbert Humbert destroys Lolita's attempt of self-identification not giving her a chance. She is only twelve years old when they meet for the first time.

While, in *Bonjour Tristesse,* Raymond lets his daughter make her own experiences with boys in total freedom so that she finds true love one day, Humbert Humbert, on the contrary, takes away any possibility for Lolita of experiencing normal teenage love by imposing on her a horrible toxic and invasive relationship. Lolita does have some kind of affair with another younger man called Charlie but this never develops into anything constructive. Lolita will have a disastrous emotional future, alone and pregnant, she will die young. If the name Lolita has become the archetype of a young nymphet who plays with the attractiveness of her body, in the novel the portrait is much less sexy because, Dolores (Lolita's real name) is quite a simple and ordinary girl. The film produced by Stanley Kubrick, emphasises and exaggerates Lolita's perverse behaviour which is not expressed in quite the same way in the novel.

In *The Graduate*, written by Charles Webb in 1963, we have the same kind of toxic love between an adult and a teenager but this time the roles are reversed. When Benjamin Braddock graduates from a small Eastern college and moves back to his parent's house on the West Coast, everyone wants to know what he is going to do with his life. Embittered by the emptiness of his college education and indifferent to his grim prospects, Benjamin seems quite lost, spending the summer deciding what he wants to do with his life, wandering around rather aimlessly. Despite being well educated and enjoying the privileges of his upper middle class upbringing, he doesn't know which direction to take. In fact, the prospect of a career seems to contribute significantly to Benjamin's discomfort. He wants to transcend the corporate scripts followed by his parents, but he doesn't really know how to achieve this.

Benjamin rebels against his parent's obsession of him finding a professional path 'in the plastics industry.' They keep on pestering him to meet their friends and settle down:

The very beginning of the novel sets the picture:

> "His father called up from the foot of the stairs but there was no answer. Finally he hurried up the stairs to the end of the hall.
>
> "Ben?" he said opening his son's door.
>
> "I'll be down later" Benjamin said.
>
> "Ben, the guests are all here," his father said "they are waiting."
>
> "I said I'll be down later."
>
> Mr Braddock closed the door behind him. "What is it?" he said. Benjamin shook his head and walked to the window.

"What is it Ben?"

"Nothing."

"Then why don't you come down and see your guests?"

Benjamin didn't answer.

"Ben?"

"Dad" he said turning round, "I have some thing on my mind right now."

"What things?"

"Just some things"

"Well can't you just tell me what they are?"

"No."

Mr Braddock continued frowning at his son for a few minutes, glanced at his watch, then looked at Benjamin. "Ben, these are our friends down there," he said. "My friends. Your mother's friends. You owe them a little curtesy."

"Tell them I have to be alone right now."

Benjamin needs the psychological and social moratorium that was mentioned earlier on. His reaction against his parents is a combination of provocation and opposition against conformity, firstly he just wants to be left alone and later his rebellion takes the shape of the relationship he accepts with a woman much older than himself and who is a friend of the family. Mrs Robinson's sexual advances provide an outlet for Benjamin in a wayward period. Later on, he will turn against Mrs Robinson who was starting to play the double role of a mistress and of an overprotective and directive mother, by marrying her daughter. The relationship with Mrs Robinson's lacks communication for Benjamin who needs to talk to her to understand what is going on in her mind and ultimately in his. In his farewell note, he mentions that lack of dialogue:

> I don't know if you were ever taught the difference between right and wrong or not, but since I was, I feel a certain obligation to it and cannot continue in as devious a fashion as I have been. Since we never exactly lose ourselves in conversation, I'm not sure how you feel about things but obviously what we are doing can only lead to some kind of disaster if we go on...

At the beginning Benjamin refuses to go out with Elaine, Mrs Robinson's daughter, precisely because his parents want him to. He later discovers that she is not only pretty but very intelligent and understanding. She also shares Benjamin's desire to escape their predictable suburban futures, running from her own wedding to embark on an uncertain future with an imperfect partner. While she could have married the conscientious and responsible Carl, she chooses Benjamin on a whim, trusting their intellectual and philosophical connection more than her drive for security.

Benjamin's letter to her has all the intensity of adolescent love:

Dear Elaine,

I love you and I can't help myself and I am begging you to forgive me for what I did. I love you so much I am terrified of seeing you every time I step out the door, I cringe in terror that you will be there please help me please forget what I did…

Unlike Lolita, Benjamin manages to drag himself away from the overpowering Mrs Robinson, mainly because of the return of Elaine, who coincides perfectly with the kind of teenage love he was looking for. What is interesting is that Benjamin feels the need to talk to Mrs Robinson, whereas she is just using him as a sex object, depriving him of the cognitive analysis of what is going on in his confused mind.

Not long after Stanley Kubrick's cinematographic success with *Lolita* in 1962, *The Graduate* directed by Mike Nichols was also acclaimed as a great film in 1967.

Identity crisis in adolescence happens when teenagers are trying to make the rights choices in life but they can't really understand whether it's because they want to or because they are trying to satisfy their parents. This kind of adolescent identity was played out by James Dean in *Rebel Without a Cause*. The book that served for the title of the movie does not have much to do with it. The original title is *Rebel Without a Cause: The Hypnoanalysis of a Criminal Psychopath*, written by psychiatrist Robert M. Lindner. But the theme of the movie adaptation is worth analysing.

It is the drama of emotionally confused suburban, middle-class teenagers. They are all portrayed as frustrated because of the dysfunctions of their respective families. Jim

Stark (James Dean) feels anguished by his constantly bickering parents, his mother being too manipulative and his father being too passive. Judy feels that her father ignores her because she is no longer a little girl, and Plato is abandoned by his father and does not see his mother much. Unconsciously, he would like Jim to become his new father, or at least to take his role.

To get more attention, Judy dresses in a provocative way and explains to the officer Ray, how she feels.

> Judy: "He calls me a tramp – my own father!"
> Ray: "Do you think he really means that?"
> Judy: "Yes! I don't know! Maybe he doesn't mean it but he acts like he does."

They all get involved in mischief with a gang of delinquents led by a young man called Buzz. The title is significant because it refers to the fact that youngsters rebel against things that might not be that important, or that will or could subside with time and thought. The consequences of their acts can be disastrous, as Buzz is killed during a challenge and Plato accidentally dies because of a misunderstanding. It also shows the tension between desire and ability and how teenagers interact with each other. As they are not able to express what they feel, they resort to brutality and fighting. This violence has the opposite effect, and undermines their wish to be taken seriously. I find this title characteristic of teenager's rebellion and agitation which does fizzle out with time and maturity but which must be given all the attention it can get to avoid tragedy.

L'Amant (*The Lover*) written by Margarite Duras in 1984 is also fascinating. Here, the main character is a young girl of sixteen living in the French colony of Indochina in the 1930s, who throws herself in a physical interracial relationship at a period of time when this was not acceptable. What makes the interest of this novel, according to me, is the juxtaposition of the experience of a teenager and the detached narrative of the same teenager who has become an adult. The use of the third person mixed with first person narrative shows the reader simultaneously the experience of the young girl and the recounting of the same story by the same person who has become a mature woman. An identical event narrated by different points of view, one obsession seen through the prism of different people and interpretations. One event narrated or interpreted by different people. In this case the love making between the teenager and her lover. The heroine is fifteen years old when she gets involved in an affair with a Chinese man of thirty-six. What seems to be at the start only a physical relationship will reveal itself as being much more, but the teenager will take a very long time to acknowledge this: *'L'avoir aimé d'un amour qu'elle n'avait pas vu.'* ('To have loved him with a love that she hadn't seen.')

So what pushed this young girl to make love to a man twenty-one years older and belonging to the Chinese community? Here again, it was the behaviour of her demanding and authoritative mother who had little if no love for her daughter. She wanted to get rid of a chaotic family background, she started by dressing differently from other schoolgirls, then started a passionate and forbidden physical relationship in a world that was new to her, made of violent emotions. Transgression, refusal of a stifling family atmosphere, everything will push her in the arms of a lover who is hardly a person at that early stage. He has no name, only a function being an outlet like a personal diary which she uses to liberate herself. Here, just like in *Bonjour Tristesse,* there is a total refusal of conformism. Paradoxically, what the reader is left with at the end of the novel, is the beauty of the relationship between two people that seem to have nothing in common. The love which was born from a desire to rebel ends in being poignantly authentic. I recall having seen the 1992 movie produced by Jean-Jacques Annaud with Jane March and Tony Leung Ka-fai which made me want to read the book. Both the original text and the adaptation are masterpieces in my opinion.

Let's move from Indochina to the United States with Carson McCullers, an American author. She managed what is most difficult in the description of teenagers in fiction, that is it to illustrate all the complexity of their contradictory desires. Being able to show simultaneously their desire of individualism and their need for belonging is a real challenge. In *The Member of the Wedding*, Carson McCullers manages this brilliantly, by describing the agony of adolescence.

In a little town in the State of Georgia, we witness some weeks in the month of August in the life of Frankie Adams, a young girl of twelve. Frankie was raised by a widowed father who is distant and quite absent from her life and by Berenice, an Afro-American maid who tries to put her back into place whenever she shows signs of irrational behaviour. Frankie is the epitome of an alienated teenager. Up to this point she has been a tomboy, a carefree and headstrong child. She feels inexplicably lost when her body begins to change. She is even 'afraid' she has no one to explain the natural changes that are occurring to her She looks more like a boy, tall, lanky and awkward in her thin body. She has just cut her blond hair off and find herself in conflict with everything around her, including herself. Her own body seems to fit nowhere. 'This summer she was grown so tall that she was almost a big freak and her shoulders were narrow, her legs too long.'

Despite the extremely limited number of actual events taking place during that summer, those few days mark a turning point in the young girl's existence. Frankie is on the cusp of adolescence but not quite severed from childhood yet. McCullers captures her state of "in-between-ness". She cannot go back to childhood and she is uncertain how to advance into adolescence. The irony of the novel is that Frankie is breaking away in her mind, imagining herself as a grownup when, to others, she is still clearly a child.

In a 1956 interview, Carson McCullers answered a journalist's question: 'What are your characters looking for?' with 'They need to belong to something.' The title itself is relevant, *The Member of a Wedding*. Precisely, Frankie feels that she does not belong anywhere. The other children seem too young to her but she does not fit in with the older girls either. She also feels that she is going nowhere that she is somehow trapped. She feels that 'the world seems somehow separate from herself.'

The story

> ... happened that green and crazy summer when Frankie was twelve years old. This was the summer when for a long time she had not been a member. She belonged to no club and was a member of nothing in the world.

The irony of the novel is that Frankie is breaking away in her mind, imagining herself as a grown up when, to others, she is still clearly a child. Frankie is stuck in the torpor and immobility of her youth and she thinks that she has found the solution to her existential wandering by using her brother's wedding as a kind of personal opportunity for salvation. She thinks that she will be able to take part in the wedding by sharing with the newlyweds their honeymoon in Alaska, thus escaping her life that doesn't make much sense to her. She unconsciously believes that the construction of her identity is going to take shape if she takes part in a project which, *de facto*, she will never be able to be part of. Indeed, how can one be a member of a wedding if not the bridesmaid or the groom?

But when she talks about the wedding she finally feels connected to people. She has the impression of belonging to a larger group at last, a group of adults. She is set back temporarily when the wedding couple rejects her; however, Frankie remains determined and at the end of the novel she plans to escape from her limited life.

She writes in a letter:

Dear Father,

This is a farewell letter until I write you from a different place. I told you I was going to leave town because it is inevitable. I cannot stand this existence any longer because my life has become a burden. I am taking the pistol because who can tell when it might come in handy and I will send back the money to you at the very first opportunity. Tell Berenice not to worry. The whole thing is an irony of fate and is inevitable. Later I will write. Please Papa do not try to capture me.

Sincerely yours,
Frances Addams

We can find another teenager escaping in *The Catcher in the Rye* (1951), a novel written by famous American writer J.D. Salinger. It is the story of a high-school boy growing up in the world of decadent New York. Holden Caulfield is also on the journey from childhood to adulthood. His adolescent problems include protection of innocence and disgust for the phoniness of the adult world. Holden behaves erratically and impulsively and has negative attitudes towards almost everything.

He is expelled from school because of his poor academic performance and is afraid to meet his parents earlier than they were expecting him so he decides to stay in the New York City Hotel. He meets many adults he does not get on with. Then he decides to go West and spend the rest of his life there. When he goes to say goodbye to his sister Phoebe, she insists on going with him. This unexpected act of love drives him out of his dream and his nightmarish three-day adventure in New York. Finally he goes home, falls ill, and recovers in a psychiatric ward in California. It is there that he recounts his sad story of growing up.

The title of the book — *The Catcher in the Rye* — first appears in Chapter 16, when a kid is singing the Robert Burns song "Comin' Thro' the Rye". In Chapter 22, when Phoebe asks Holden what he wants to do with his life, Holden tells his sister that he would like to be a catcher in the rye: he pictures a lot of children playing in a big field of rye around the edge of a cliff. Holden imagines that he would catch them if they start to go over the cliff. His dream of becoming a "catcher in the rye" shows that Holden has affection for childhood. He wishes to save these children from danger so that they may frolic in the fields . We can interpret this as Holden's wish to save the children from the phony adult world. Holden wants to catch children before they fall out of innocence into the knowledge of the corrupted adult world.

"Phoniness" stands as an emblem of everything that's wrong in the world around the teenager and provides an excuse for him to withdraw into his cynical alienation. Throughout the novel, Holden seems to be excluded from and victimised by the world around him. Holden likes the world to be silent and frozen, predictable and unchanging. Even so, Holden still desperately continues searching for new relationships, but always avoiding any involvement at the last moment. Holden's loneliness, a more concrete manifestation of his alienation problem, is a driving force throughout the book. Most of the novel describes his almost maniac quest for companionship as he flits from one meaningless encounter to another.

We can see that Holden never expresses his own emotions directly, nor does he attempt to discover the source of his troubles. He desperately needs human contact, care, and love, but his protective wall prevents him from obtaining them.

Holden Caulfield is an unusual protagonist for a Bildungsroman because his central goal is to resist the process of maturity itself. As his thoughts about the Museum of Natural History demonstrate, Holden fears change and is overwhelmed by complexity. He wants everything to be easily understandable and eternally fixed, like the statues of Eskimos and Indians in the museum. He is frightened because he is guilty of the sins he criticises in others, and because he can't understand everything around him. But he refuses to acknowledge this fear, expressing it only in a few instances: for example when he talks about sex and admits that 'sex is something I just don't understand. I swear to God I don't.'

Holden seems to have a fixed idea that adulthood is a world of superficiality and hypocrisy, while childhood is a world of innocence, curiosity, and honesty and he stubbornly negates any possibility of passage from one world to the other.

Moving back to Europe, in Italy in the 1950s, we have *L'Amica Geniale* written by Elena Ferrante. Two friends, Elena and Lila, live in a poor district of the town, their families have no money and, although they have intellectual potential and could do well at school, it is not the path that is going to be given to them. Lila who is the most intelligent one, soon gives up school to work with her father and her brother in their shoe mender's shop. On the other hand, Elena is coached and supported by her teacher who push her parents to send her to college like the children of the Caracci and the Sarratore, wealthier families who can afford education for their children.

What is fascinating in this novel is the psychological and physical transformation of the two girls who alternatively help or attack each other. Their winding paths sometimes run parallel or apart. They will finally reach adulthood having gone through suffering and breakups. *L'Amica Geniale* is the portrayal of two unforgettable characters that Elena Ferrante follows with passion and tenderness deep into their soul.

I am not nostalgic of our childhood, it was full of violence... It was life and that's all, and we grew up with the obligation of rendering it difficult to others before they made it impossible for us.

This violence makes me think of a short story, or novella, published in 1930 by Irène Némirovsky, a writer of Russian origin who was successful between the two wars. "The Ball" portrays an adolescent in the 1920s called Antoinette Kampf.

> She was a tall flat girl of 14 years of age, with the pale complexion of that age, with so little flesh that she appeared, to the eyes of adults, like a round blank spot, without any traits, lowered eye-lids, with dark circles, a little closed mouth (...) fourteen, breasts growing under her tight school dress and that seem to harm and hinder her feeble body, childlike. (...) Big feet and those long flute like limbs with red hands at the end of them, fingers covered in ink, and that may become , who knows? the most beautiful arms. (...) A fragile neck, short hair, with no colour, dry and thin...

Antoinette is bullied by her mother, a woman of strong personality and incapable of the slightest tenderness towards her daughter. The father is a rich banker who is quite absent and who has not true relevance in the story. Here again, it is the maid who looks after the teenager. The mother refuses to let her daughter take part in the first ball that she and her husband want to organise. The young girl is hurt and frustrated and wants to take revenge on this total absence of understanding on her mother's part.

When she goes out with her nanny, her mother asks her to put all the invitations to the ball in the post box. The young girl agrees, but instead of doing so, she throws all the letters in the River Seine.

On the night of the ball, no one shows up apart from Antoinette's piano teacher, an old woman who is surly and authoritative. Mrs Kampf is distraught. Her daughter comes to console her. That is the precise moment when the young girl has the impression of becoming an adult. 'She stepped back, looked at herself with a happy smile… life was beginning, finally! Maybe this very evening?'

"The Ball" is an exquisite recounting of a crisis which explores the passage from childhood to adulthood. The novella seems to be largely autobiographical, showing the transposition of the author's own conflict with her unloving mother, just as she also portrayed her in "The Enemy".

As well as other texts written in later years, the violent sorrows that Antoinette addresses to her mother Rosine show that all of Némirovsky's literary production is unable to quench the thirst for love that she felt and that apparently, her mother never managed to give her.

> Having to wait… and these bad wishes… why such shameful desires, desperate, that eat up the heart when one sees two lovers at dusk kissing while walking and stumbling like if they were drunk… An old maid's hate at fourteen? She well knows that she will have her share; but it is so long. It is as though it will never happen, and, in the meantime, life is narrow, humiliating, lessons, harsh discipline, mother who is shouting…

I would like to conclude with a passage from the well-known novel by Harper Lee, *To Kill a Mockingbird* (1960). The family circle is composed of a widower, Atticus, and his two children Scout and Jem; the female character who looks after and educates the children is Calpurnia, an Afro-American, just as in McCullers' novel. What is admirable about this novel in my opinion is the empathic teaching that the father gives his children and which is a real lesson of life. While defending a black man wrongly accused of raping a white girl, he tells them 'You never really understand a person until you consider things from his point of view until you climb into his skin and walk around it.'

Could it be that ultimately, understanding adolescents would be to put oneself in their shoes if not try to remember what we went through when we were their age? And instead of wanting to change and improve our teenagers, shouldn't we try to save what is left of our own adolescence to cherish the best of it? It is the very meaning of the famous poem "Youth" by Samuel Ullman, poet and American business-man, who died in 1924. A poem that every adult should know.

YOUTH

Youth is not a time of life – it is a state of mind,
It is a temper of the will,
A quality of the imagination,
A vigour of the emotions,
A predominance of courage over timidity,
Of the appetite for adventure over love of ease.

Nobody grows old by merely living a number of years.
People grow old only by deserting their ideals.
Years wrinkle the skin,
But to give up enthusiasm wrinkles the soul.
Worry, doubt, self-distrust,
Fear and despair – these are the long,
Long years that bow the head and
Turn the growing spirit back to dust.

Whether they are sixteen or seventy,
There is in every being's heart
The love of wonder,
The sweet amazement at the stars
And star like things and thoughts,
The undaunted challenge of events,
The unfailing childlike appetite
For what is to come next,
And the joy and the game of life.

You are as young as your faith,
As old as your doubt;
As young as your self-confidence,
As old as your fear,
As young as your hope,
As old as your despair.

When the wires are all down
And all the innermost core of your heart
Is covered with the snows of pessimism
And the ice of cynicism,
Then you are grown old indeed.

But so long as your heart receives messages
Of beauty, cheer, courage, grandeur
And power from the earth,
From man and from the Infinite,
So long you are young.

Samuel Ullman

BIBLIOGRAPHY

Amato, Paul R.; Fowler, Frieda. "Parenting Practices, Child Adjustment, and Family Diversity", in: *Journal of Marriage and Family*. 64. August 2002. pp. 703–716.

Armbrester, Margaret England. *Samuel Ullman and Youth: The life, the Legacy.* The University of Alabama Press. Tuscaloosa, 2009.

Austen, Jane. *The Complete Novels.* Book Club Associates BCA. London, 1995.
— T*eenage Writings*, Oxford World's Classics. Oxford, 2017.

Baumrind, Diana. "Child care practices anteceding three patterns of preschool behavior", in: *Genetic Psychology Monographs, 75(1)*, 1967. pp. 43–88.

Briggs Myers, Isabel and Peter. *Gifts differing. Understanding Personality Type.* Davies Black Publishing. California, 1995.

Britton, Clare. "Children who cannot play" in: *New Educational Fellowship Monograph*. 3, November, 1945. pp. 12–27.

Brontë, Charlotte. *Jane Eyre.* (Originally published in 1847.) Penguin Classics. London, 2006.

Cline, Foster; MD and Fay, Jim. *Parenting Teens with Love and Logic. Preparing Adolescents for Responsible Adulthood.* Updated and expanded edition. NavPress. Colorado Springs, 2006

HH Dalai-Lama and Cutler, Howard C. *The Art of Happiness*. Easton Press. Norwalk, 1998.

Davis. Heather. *The Elementary School Journal. (Exploring the contexts of relationship*

quality between Middle School Students and Teachers.) Vol. 106. No. 3. The University of Chicago Press. Chicago, 2006. pp. 193–223.

Erikson, Erik H. *Childhood and Society*. 2d ed., rev. W.W. Norton. New York, 1963 (first edition: 1950).
— *Identity: Youth and Crisis*. The University of Michigan. W.W Norton & Company. New York, 1968.
— *Identity and the Life Circle*. W.W. Norton & Company, International Universities Press, Inc. New York, 1994.
— *Life Cycle Completed*. W.W. Norton & Company. New York, 1998.

Findlay, Leanne and Bowker, Anne. "The Link between Competitive Sport Participation and Self-Concept in Early Adolescence: A Consideration of Gender and Sport Orientation", in: *Journal of Youth and Adolescence*. 38. Jan. 2009, pp. 29–40.

Freud, Sigmund. *The Interpretation of Dreams*. 3rd edition. Translated by A. A. Brill. The Macmillan Company. New York, 1913.

Giedd, Jay. "Brain Development during Childhood and Adolescence. A Longitudinal Study", in: *Nature Neuroscience. 2 (10)*. 1999. pp. 861–863.

Goleman, Daniel. *Emotional Intelligence*. Bloomsbury. London, 1995.
— *Working with Emotional Intelligence*. Bloomsbury. London, 1998.

Grasha, Anthony F. "A Matter of Style: The Teacher as Expert, Formal Authority, Personal Model, Facilitator, and Delegator", in: College Teaching, Vol. 42, No. 4 (Fall, 1994), pp. 142-149.

Hao, Lingxin, V. Joseph Hotz, and Ginger Zhe Jin. "Games Parents and Adolescents Play: Risky Behaviors, Parental Reputation, and Strategic Transfers", (2005), in: Economic Journal 118, 528 (April 2008). pp. 515–555.

Hardy, Thomas. *Tess of the D'Ubervilles. A Pure Woman.* (Originally published in 1891) Penguin. London, 1990.

Hersch, Patricia. *A Tribe Apart. A Journey into the Heart of American Adolescence.* Fawcett Columbine. New York,1998.

Huitt, W. "Self and self-views" [archive], in: *Educational Psychology Interactive*, Valdosta State University. Valdosta, GA, 2011.

Goethe, Johann Wolfgang von. *Wilhelm Meister's Apprenticeship.* (Originally published in 1795-1895.) Translation from German by Thomas Carlyle. Kessinger Publishing Co. Whitefish, 2008.

Dr Jensen, Frances E. *The Teenage Brain. A Neuroscientist's Survival Guide to Raising*

Adolescents and Young Adults. Harper Collins. New York, 2016.

Joyce, James. *Portrait of an Artist as a Young Man.* B. W. Huebsch. New York, 1916.

Jung, Carl Gustav. *Collected Works. Psychology Types.* (Originally published in 1920.) Routledge & Kegan Paul. London and Henley, 1978.

Keirsley, David and Bates, Marilyn. *Please Understand Me II. Character and temperament types.* Prometheus Nemesis Book Co. Del Mar, 1998. (originally published in 1978).

Klein, Melanie. *The Psychoanalysis of Children.* W W Norton & Co. New York, 1932.

Korczak, Janusz. *How to love a child* (Originally published as *Jak kochać dziecko*, Warsaw, 1919) *[: in honour of the centenary of Janusz Korczak 1878-1978]*, Polish Committee for the Janusz Korczak Centenary, 1978.
— *When I Am Little Again* and *The Child's Right to Respect.* (Originally published in 1925 and 1929.) Translated from the Polish by E. P. Kulawiec. University Press of America. Lanham, 1992.

Lawrence, David Herbert. *Sons and Lovers*, Wordsworth Classics. Ware, 1992.

Lee, Harper. *To Kill a Mockingbird.* J. B. Lippincott & Co. Philadelphia, 1960.

Dr. Leman, Kevin. *Birth Order Book: Why You Are the Way You Are.* Revel, a division of Baker Publishing Group. Baker Publishing Group. Grand Rapids, 1998.

Lindner, Robert M. *Rebel Without a Cause: The Hypnoanalysis of a Criminal Psychopath*, Grune & Stratton Inc. New York, 1953.

Locke, John. *Some Thoughts Concerning Education.* (Originally published in 1693.) Oxford University Press, Clarendon Press. Oxford, 1989.

Maccoby, Eleanor E. and Martin, John A. "Socialization in the context of the family: Parent-child interaction". In: Mussen, Paul H.; Hetherington, E. M. *Manual of child psychology, Vol. 4: Social development.* John Wiley and Sons. New York, 1983

Marche, Stephen. *How Shakespeare Changed Everything.* Harper. New York, 2011.

Marcia, James E. "Development and Validation of Ego-Identity Status", in: *Journal of Personality and Social Psychology*, Vol.3, no. 5, 1996.
— "Ego-Identity Status", in: Argyle, Michael. *Social Encounters*. Penguin. London, 1977. pp. 340–354

Marsh, Herbert W. and Martin, Andrew J., "Academic self-concept and academic achievement: Relations and causal ordering", in: *British Journal of Educational Psychology* vol. 81, no 1, 2011, pp. 59–77.

Maruscsak, Lance. "What are the Effects of the Self-Concept Theory in High school Students?" (http://people.wcsu.edu/mccarneyh/acad/Maruscsak.html) Western Connecticut State University, 2012.

Mayeroff, Milton. *On Caring*. Harper & Row. New York, 1971.

McCullers, Carson. *The Member of the Wedding*. Houghton Mifflin. Boston, 1946.

Mitchell, Margaret. *Gone with the Wind*. Macmillan Publishers USA. New York, 1936.

Musil, Robert. *The Man Without Qualities (…)*. (Originally published between 1930 and 1943), Translated from German by Willa Muir. 3 volumes. Secker and Warburg. London, 1953, 1954, and 1960.

Nabokov, Vladimir. *Lolita*. Olympia Press. Paris, 1955.

Neill, Alexander Sutherland. *Summerhill School: a New View of Childhood*. St Martin's Griffin. New York, 1995.

Noddings, Nel. *Caring: A Feminine Approach to Ethics and Moral Education*. Berkeley University of California Press. Berkeley, 1984.
— *The Challenge to Care in Schools. An Alternative Approach to*

Education. Advances in Contemporary Educational Thought series, vol. 8. Teachers' College Press, New York, 1992.

— *Caregiving: Readings in Knowledge, Practice, Ethics and Politics* (co-edited with Suzanne Gordon, Patricia E. Benner). Studies in Health, Illness and Caregiving in America. University of Pennsylvania Press, Philadelphia, 1996.

— *Uncertain Lives: Children of Promise, Teachers of Hope* (co-author with Robert V. Bullough) Teachers' College Press. New York, 2001.

— *Starting at Home: Caring and Social Policy.* Berkeley, University of California Press. Berkeley, 2002.

— *A Richer Brighter Vision for American High Schools.* Cambridge University Press. Cambridge, 2015.

Rogers, Carl Ransom. *Freedom to Learn.* Charles E. Merrill. Columbus, 1969.

Rubie-Davies, Christine M., "Teacher Expectations and Student Self-Perceptions: Exploring

Relationships", in: *Psychology in the Schools,* vol. 43, no 5, May 2006, pp. 537–552.

Sadhwani, Indu. "Effect of Self-Concept on Adolescent Depression", in: *Journal of Psychosocial Research.* 7, Spring 2012. pp. 147–52.

Salinger, Jerome David. *The Catcher in the Rye.* Little Book Group USA, Brown and Company. Boston, 1951.

Shakespeare, William. *Romeo and Juliet.* (First published in 1597.) Penguin Classics. London, 2015.

— *A Midsummer Night's Dream.* (First published in 1600.) Penguin Classics. London, 2015.

— *Hamlet.* (First published around 1602.) Penguin Classics. London, 2015.

— *King Lear.* (First published 1608.) Penguin Classics. London, 2015.

— *All's Well That Ends Wells.* (First published in 1623.) Penguin Classics. London, 2015.

Sophocles. *Antigone.* Peguin Classics. London, 2015.

Stanley Hall, Granville. *Adolescence.* Appleton and Company. New York, 1907.

Steinbeck, John. *A life in Letters.* Edited by Elaine Steinbeck and Robert Wallsten. Vicking. New York, 1975.

Stevick, Richard A. *Growing up Amish, The Teenage Years.* Second edition. John Hopkins University Press. Baltimore, 2014.

Tarcov, Nathan. *Locke's Education for Liberty.* University of Chicago Press. Chicago, 1984.

Teuber, Andreas. "Simone Weil: Equality as Compassion." In: Philosophy and Phenomenological Research 43, no. 2, 1982. pp. 221–237.

Tyler, Anne. "Teenage Wasteland." In: Carver, Raymond (ed.), *The Best American Short stories.* Houghton Mifflin Harcourt. Boston, 1986.

Webb, Charles. *The Graduate.* New American Library. New York, 1963.

Winnicott, Donald. *Thinking about Children.* London Perseus Press, 1996.
— "Hate in the counter-transference.", *in: Journal of psychotherapy practice and research* vol. 3,4 (1994): pp. 348-56.

Yolton, John. *John Locke and Education.* Random House. New York, 1971.

—

Anouilh, Jean. *Le Bal des Voleurs*. Fayard, Paris, 1938.

Aries, Phillippe. *L'enfant et la Vie familiale sous l'Ancien Régime*. Seuil. Paris, 1975.

Baker, Caroline. *Insoumission à l'École obligatoire*. Édition Tahin Parly. Lyon, 2008.

De Beauvoir, Simone. *Mémoires d'une Jeune Fille Rangée*. Gallimard. Paris, 1956.

Birraux, Annie. *Le Corps Adolescent*. Bayard Culture. Montrouge, 2004.
— *L'adolescent Face à son corps*. Albin Michel. Paris, 1990.

Bourdillon, François (dir.). *Rapport Annuel 2017*. Santé Publique France. Saint Maurice, 2017.

Chrétien de Troyes. *Lancelot ou Le chevalier à la Charrette*. Traduction de Daniel Poirion. Folio. 133, Gallimard. Paris, 2008.

Cicchelli, Vincenzo. "Les legs du voyage de formation à la *Bildung* cosmopolite", in: *Le Télémaque*, vol. 38, no. 2, 2010, pp. 57–70.

Corneille, Pierre. *Le Cid*. (Originally published in 1637.) Hachette. Paris, 1986.

Dolto, Françoise. *La Cause des Enfants*. Robert Laffont. Paris, 1985.
— *La Cause des Adolescents*. Robert Laffont. Paris, 1988.
— *Paroles pour Adolescents ou le complexe du Homard*. Hatier. Paris, 1989.
— *Les Chemins de l'Education*. Gallimard. Paris, 1994.

Dumas, Alexandre. *Lettres à mon fils. Le temps retrouvé*. Mercure de France. Paris, 2008.

Duras, Marguerite. *L'Amant.* Les éditions de Minuit. Paris, 1984.

Erikson, Erik H. *Adolescence et Crises. La quête de l'identité.* Champs Flammarion Sciences. Paris, 1994.

Hugo, Victor. *Les Misérables.* (Originally published in 1862.) Pocket classiques. Paris, 2016.

Langevin, Brigitte. *Aider mon Enfant à Mieux Dormir. De la Naissance à l'Adolescence.* Editions de Mortagne. Boucherville, 2009.

Le Breton, David. *En Souffrance. Adolescence et Entrée dans la Vie.* Métaillé. Paris, 2007.
— *Cultures Adolescentes. Entre turbulence et construction de soi.* Autrement. Paris, 2008.

Lehalle, Henry. *Psychologie des Adolescents.* Coll. Le Psychologue. P.U.F. Paris, 1991

Marty, François. "Adolescence et Émotion, une Affaire de Corps" in: *Enfance & Psy,* vol.49, n°4, 2010, pp. 40–52.

Masdonati, Jonas et Lamamra. *Arrêter une formation professionnelle.* Collection: Existences et Société, édit. Antipodes. Lausanne, 2009.

Mathelin, Catherine and Costa, Bernadette. *Comment survivre en famille.* Albin Michel Jeunesse. Paris, 2002.

Némirovsky, Irène. *Le Bal.* In: *Les Œuvres libres,* 1929.

P. Périer, "L'enfant entre deux mondes: disqualification parentale et autonomisation scolaire", in: *Les Sciences de l'Éducation,* Vol. 48, 2015/1, Ed. Cerce, Université de Caen; et PUF, coll. Éducation et société. Paris, 2014.
— "La réaffiliation scolaire d'élèves de lycée professionnel.

Contribution à une analyse des pratiques enseignantes dans les classes difficiles." In: *Carrefours de l'éducation*. 2008/2 (no.22)

Perrault, Charles. *Peau d'âne*, in: *Contes de ma Mère l'Oye* (Originally published in 1694.) Folioplus Classique, Paris, 2006.

Piaget, Jean et Inhelder, Bärbel. *La Psychologie de l'Enfant*. P.U.F. Paris, 1966

De Pixerécourt, René-Charles Guilbert. *Coélina ou l'Enfant du Mystère*. (Originally published in 1800.) Hachette BNF. Paris, 2015.

Pommereau, Xavier. *Quand L'adolescent Va Mal. L'écouter, le comprendre, l'aimer*. Editions Jean-Claude Lattès, Paris, 1997.
— *Le Goût du Risque à l'Adolescence. Le comprendre et l'accompagner*. Albin Michel. Paris, 2016.
— *Ado à Fleur de Peau. Ce que révèle son apparence*. Albin Michel. Paris, 2006.

L'abbé Prévost, Antoine François. *Histoire de Manon Lescaut*. (Originally published in 1731.) La Nouvelle bibliothèque. La Chaux-de-Fonds, 1948.

Racine. *Iphigénie*. (Originally published in 1674.) Hachette. Paris, 2007.

Rimbaud, Arthur. *Poésies. Une Saison en Enfer. Illuminations*. (Originally published in, respectively, 1895, 1973 and 1895.) Folio Classique. Paris, 2017.

Rousseau, Jean Jacques. Émile, ou de l'Éducation. (Originally published in 1762) Flammarion, Format Poche, Paris, 2009

Sagan, Françoise. *Bonjour Tristesse. Éd*. Julliard. Paris, 1954

Van Gennep, Arnold. *Les Rites de Passage*. E. Nourry. Paris, 1909

Virat, Mael. *Dimension affective de la relation enseignant-élève: effet sur l'adaptation psychosociale des adolescents (motivations, empathie, adaptation scolaire et violence) et rôle déterminant de l'amour compassionnel des enseignants*. (Thèse). Université Paul Valéry. Montpellier III, 2014.

Watkins, Kevin *et alia*. *La situation des enfants dans le monde 2016. L'égalité des chances pour chaque enfant*. UNICEF. New York, 2016.

Weil, Simone. La Pesanteur et la Grâce. Librairie Plon. Paris, 1947.

Zola, Émile. *Nana*. Folio Classique. (Originally published in 1880.) Paris, 2002.

—

Ferrante, Elena. *L'Amica Geniale*. Collection Dal Mondo. Editioni E/O. Rome, 2011.

Morante, Elsa. *L'Isola di Arturo Collana*. Einaudi. Torino, 1957.

Moravia, Alberto. *La Disubbidienza*. Editore Bompiani. Milano, 1948.
— *Agostino*. Editore Bompiani. Milano, 1944.

CPSIA information can be obtained
at www.ICGtesting.com
Printed in the USA
BVHW071943110819
555624BV00002B/591/P